TEEN
Triple P
Group
Workbook

EMOTIONAL BEHAVIOUR

Alan Ralph PhD
Matthew R. Sanders PhD

- Arrive on time

- Do not

N

Published by
Triple P International Pty. Ltd. ABN 17 079 825 817
PO Box 1300
Milton QLD 4064
Website: www.triplep.net

First Published 2002 Revised 2004

Copyright © 2004 The University of Queensland

Reprinted 2007, 2008, 2010

Written by Alan Ralph & Matthew R. Sanders

ISBN 978-1-876426-40-8

Designed by Australian Academic Press, Brisbane
Typeset in Goudy 10.5/12.5 by JAM Creative, Brisbane.
Cover and text design by Andrea Cox
Cartoons by Heck Lindsay

Printed by Hang Tai Printing Co Ltd

Contents

Acknowledgments

The Positive Parenting Program for Parents of Teenagers (Teen Triple P) is an initiative of the Parenting and Family Support Centre at The University of Queensland. Teen Triple P builds on the highly successful Triple P for parents of infants, toddlers, preschool and primary school age children. It is dedicated to the many parents and teenagers who have participated in the development of the program. Many of the ideas and principles of positive parenting contained in this booklet have evolved as a result of the experience and feedback provided by parents and teenagers participating in research and therapy programs. Their assistance is gratefully acknowledged. The authors wish to acknowledge colleagues Carol Markie-Dadds and Karen Turner who contributed to the development of Triple P targeting parents of preadolescent children from which this present series evolved. We also acknowledge the financial support of the Australian Rotary Health Research Fund, Criminology Research Council, Australian Research Council, and the School of Psychology at The University of Queensland.

About the Authors

Dr Alan Ralph is Adjunct Associate Professor of Clinical Psychology at the University of Queensland. Over the past 15 years, Alan has held several clinical positions, conducted research in the area of adolescent and family problems, and written numerous articles and chapters on related topics for scientific journals and publications. He has developed programs to assist teenagers and their parents to manage problems commonly encountered during the transition into adolescence and adulthood and trained many psychologists and other practitioners to implement these programs.

Dr Matt Sanders is Professor of Clinical Psychology and Director of the Parenting and Family Support Centre at The University of Queensland. Over the past 25 years, Matt has gained an international reputation for scientific research into the family-based treatment and prevention of behavioural and emotional problems in children. He has written numerous articles on parent training and evidence-based family interventions for scientific journals and authored several books on the treatment of children's behaviour problems, including the popular parenting book *Every Parent: A Positive Approach to Children's Behaviour*.

The authors have combined their research and clinical experience to develop Teen Triple P specifically for parents of teenagers. This has involved writing parenting tip sheets and workbooks, as well as professional training programs and manuals. They also conduct skills training workshops for parents, and health, education and welfare professionals. Their hands-on assistance to families has guided the development of programs to manage common developmental issues and child and teenager behaviour problems such as disobedience, aggression, peer relationship problems, school-based difficulties, family conflict, and other everyday difficulties experienced by parents and teenagers.

Introduction

The Positive Parenting Program for parents of teenagers (Teen Triple P) aims to make parenting easier. This workbook offers suggestions and ideas on positive parenting to help you promote your teenager's development.

Many parents approach the prospect of their children becoming teenagers with some apprehension and the teenage years certainly bring many challenges for all concerned. Teenagers have to cope with many physical changes to their bodies as they go through puberty. Sexual maturation occurs at different times and this can make them very self-conscious and sensitive to comments. The move into high school brings increasing demands for independence and responsibility. Teenagers are expected to make more decisions for themselves. This includes being more self-directed with schoolwork, and developing their own beliefs about who they are and what they want to do with their lives. They are also exposed to a range of widely differing and conflicting views and opinions from peers, teachers, parents, and the media. Sometimes teenagers may be tempted to experiment in ways that might put their health or future prospects at risk. Some risk-taking is normal and short-lived, but it can be very worrying for parents who need to monitor teenagers' behaviour closely and take action when necessary to prevent serious or long-term risk-taking.

The challenge for parents is to provide a home environment that guides and supports teenagers as they strive to become independent, well-adjusted young adults. This will often mean finding ways to deal with conflicts that may occur when the views and wishes of parents and teenagers differ. The effort required, though sometimes difficult, can lead to a close rewarding friendship between parent and teenager that provides companionship for both. There is no single right way to be a parent and there are many different views on how parents should go about raising a teenager. Ultimately, you as the parent need to develop your own approach to dealing with your teenager's behaviour. Teen Triple P has been helpful for many parents and may give you some useful ideas to help you meet the challenges of raising teenagers.

This workbook has been developed to accompany Group Teen Triple P. The program also draws on material from the booklet *Positive Parenting for Parents with Teenagers* by Dr Alan Ralph and Dr Matthew R. Sanders and the *Teen Triple P tip sheet series* which cover general parenting and specific issues relating to teenagers. During your group sessions you will watch segments of *Every Parent's Guide to Teenagers*, a DVD which provides a general overview of positive approaches to parenting with step by step explanations and demonstrations of a variety of parenting strategies.

You are invited to play an active role by participating in group sessions and completing tasks between sessions. The program has been set up to make sure you have the necessary information and skills needed to practise the strategies as soon as possible. You will be guided through the exercises in the workbook by your group leader. If you are unable to attend one of the group sessions, you can read through the material and complete the exercises in this Workbook. The tasks have been designed to further your understanding of the issues raised in each group session. They will also help you to use suggested strategies with your own family.

Your Commitment

T his program is designed to support you in your parenting role. It will require your commitment, your partnership, your time and your full participation if it is to achieve its aim. If you work through the program, you will be rewarded. As you begin reading and completing the tasks that follow, you will learn new skills and possibly new ways of thinking, acting and organising your life. If you practise these new skills and keep up your level of motivation, the program will be of more benefit to you. So, before beginning, carefully consider your level of commitment or determination to complete this program. Below you will find a declaration of intent to complete for yourself and your partner (if appropriate).

Parent one

I (name) _____ agree to play an active role throughout the program. I am able to (please tick the boxes corresponding to the aspects of the program you are able to take part in):

☐ participate in the four group sessions

☐ participate in the four telephone sessions

☐ complete set homework

Signed: _____ Date: _____

Witness: _____

Parent two (if appropriate)

I (name) _____ agree to play an active role throughout the program. I am able to (please tick the boxes corresponding to the aspects of the program you are able to take part in):

☐ participate in the four group sessions

☐ participate in the four telephone sessions

☐ complete set homework

Signed: _____ Date: _____

Witness: _____

Now that you have decided to participate, we wish you well and hope that you find the program helpful and informative.

A Few Survival Tips

All parents raising teenagers find it easier when they get support. Raising teenagers can be challenging and this task can be made less stressful if parents don't have to do it on their own.

Where there are two parents involved, discuss issues with each other, agree on discipline procedures, and support and back up each other's parenting efforts. If you have disagreements, try to deal with them when your teenager is not present, or at least reach some agreement rather than leaving it unresolved.

Other supports can be provided by family, friends, neighbours, and the parents of other teenagers. Talk about your experiences and share ideas. If you can, build up a network of the parents of your teenager's friends. This will help you to monitor what they are doing and who they are with, and to compare notes on current events.

Finally, make sure you spend time on meeting your own needs. Everyone needs to be able to get a break from parenting from time to time. Parents who find the time to do things they enjoy usually find it easier to help meet the needs of their children and teenagers.

Positive Parenting

Session 1

OVERVIEW

During Session 1 you will be given an introduction to the aims of Group Teen Triple P and what the program involves. There will be an opportunity for you to meet other parents and to share some of your experiences and ideas about being a parent. Some time will be spent discussing positive parenting as an approach to raising teenagers. You will then look at factors that influence teenagers' behaviour, set goals for change and discuss how to keep track of your teenager's behaviour.

OBJECTIVES

By the end of Session 1, you should be able to:

- describe positive parenting and what it involves
- identify factors that play a role in your teenager's behaviour patterns
- set goals for change in your teenager's and your own behaviour
- start monitoring one of your teenager's behaviours.

Working in a Group

EXERCISE 1 *Setting basic ground rules for the group*

To make sure the group runs smoothly, we need to have a few simple rules:

● Everyone needs to arrive on time and be ready to start by ....
  We will finish on time at ....

● Information about other group members should be treated confidentially and not discussed outside the group.

● Group members should be supportive of one another.

● ....
  ....
  ....
  ....

EXERCISE 2 *Getting to know you*

Share some information about yourself and your family with another group member.

EXERCISE 3 *What you would like to get out of the group sessions*

Share with the group why you are here today and what you hope to get out of this experience.

What is Positive Parenting?

Positive parenting is an approach to parenting that aims to promote teenagers' development and manage teenagers' behaviour in a constructive and non-hurtful way. It is based on good communication and positive attention to help teenagers develop the skills they need to become mature adults. Teenagers who grow up with positive parenting are likely to develop appropriate skills and feel good about themselves. They are also less likely to develop behaviour problems. There are five key aspects to positive parenting.

Ensuring a safe, engaging environment

Your teenager needs a safe but stimulating environment. As children grow older, they need to learn how to safely take on more responsibility around the home. This will include knowing how to operate gas and electrical appliances, use fire extinguishers and give basic first aid; and being competent when using power tools such as drills, saws, and mowers.

Parents also need to encourage teenagers to become involved in organised, meaningful activities at school and elsewhere, where there is appropriate adult supervision and monitoring. Appropriate supervision and monitoring of teenagers really means knowing where they are, who they are with, and what they are doing, especially when they are away from home.

Creating a positive learning environment

Older children and teenagers need to feel valued as they strive to take on adult roles and responsibilities. The best way to promote this is by gradually increasing their involvement in family decision-making. Issues will range from the relatively trivial (what name to give the new pet), to the more important (what high school to attend). Parents will still usually have the final word on many issues, especially where there may be considerable risk. Encouraging teenagers to regularly participate in discussing family issues ensures they will become skilled at making good personal decisions.

Parents need to be available to teenagers, just like when they were younger. Teenagers may have different needs and problems, but attention and encouragement are still powerful ways of signaling your approval and pleasure. When you see your teenager doing something you like, make sure you let them know. This should make it more likely they will do it again.

Using assertive discipline

When children are younger, parents tend to decide what behaviour is appropriate, and what will happen when misbehaviour occurs. As children grow into their teenage years, it is important to involve them in negotiating what the rules and responsibilities might be, and what privileges they can expect to enjoy in return.

Negotiation involves you and your teenager jointly discussing and deciding what responsibilities go with being a part of your family, and what privileges may be allowed if those responsibilities are met. This often requires compromise, trying out new arrangements, and monitoring progress. Spelling out in advance what behaviour is expected, as well as the consequences for unacceptable behaviour, can reduce conflict by helping everyone to keep calm when unacceptable teenage behaviour occurs.

Having realistic expectations

Parents' expectations of their teenagers depend on what they consider appropriate behaviour at different ages. No two teenagers are the same, and although individual differences will have generally shown up by now, additional changes in development may become noticeable during the early teenage years. The onset of puberty may affect behaviour in different ways, and peer pressure may become a major issue. It is important that you talk to other parents whenever possible to find out whether they are experiencing similar problems. Teenagers will push the limits set by parents as they see others enjoying greater apparent freedom. It is important to be realistic about the risks associated with increased teenage freedom, and ensure your teenager learns how to deal with temptations that may lead to undesirable consequences. It is also important for parents to have realistic expectations of themselves. It is fine to want to be a good parent, but to aim to be a perfect parent is setting yourself up for disappointment, for frustration, and for experiencing lots of hassles with your teenager. So be realistic. Every parent makes mistakes. Most mistakes are minor, and parents have to learn as they go along.

Taking care of yourself as a parent

Parenting is easier when personal needs for intimacy, companionship, recreation and time alone are being met. Being a good parent does not mean that your teenager should dominate your life. If your own needs as an adult are being met, it is much easier to be patient, consistent and available to your teenager.

EXERCISE 4 *What is positive parenting?*

hw

Which of these positive parenting skills do you find easy? Why?
- provide safty in home and outside
- give responsabilities
- show love & care
- sit the rules

Which of these skills do you find difficult? Why?
do not be involved (school, friends)
trust, respect, lies, screams, frustration
fair (drugs, alchool, ~~sex~~)
warring

What other things are important in helping teenagers develop?
communication, trust, Responsabilities
sports, friendship (right people)
Religion

Factors Influencing Teenagers' Behaviour

Why do teenagers behave as they do? How is it that teenagers from the same family can be so alike in some ways and so different in others? To understand how teenagers' behaviour develops, we need to consider three things — their genetic make-up, their family environment, and the community in which they live. These factors shape the skills, attitudes and abilities teenagers develop, and also influence whether they develop behaviour problems.

EXERCISE 5 *Identifying factors influencing teenagers' behaviour*

> In order to help you understand your teenager's behaviour, watch *Every Parent's Guide to Teenagers* or read through the following information.
> Place a mark next to those factors that you feel play a role in shaping your teenager's behaviour. You may also like to include some comments in the spaces provided.

Genetic Make-Up

Children inherit a unique genetic make-up from their parents. This may include physical characteristics, such as eye colour and hair texture, as well as some behavioural and emotional characteristics. For example, teenagers who have problems concentrating, or who have a tendency to feel sad or depressed may have inherited a genetic make-up that makes them more likely to have these problems.

Children may also inherit their temperament from their parents, such as how sociable or outgoing they are, how active they are, or how emotional they are. Some of these characteristics can make teenagers difficult to manage. Some of these characteristics can be quite stable and appear throughout life, while others seem to change and are replaced by others, particularly after puberty. While these factors can contribute to a teenager's problem behaviour, the way other people respond to that behaviour can also be very important.

What was your teenager like when he or she was a young child?

- demanded lots of attention ✔
- emotional and difficult to manage ☐
- very active, always on the go ☐

Comments:

When he was 1year and 9months I got another baby. That menas he was middle child. and he was jalous cryings, want me to hold him all the time especially if I care the baby, or breast feed him

The Family Environment

A person's genetic make-up is something that cannot be changed. However, children learn a lot from their family environment, and this can be changed to teach them to behave in a more appropriate way. The effects of family environment on children's behaviour are best thought of as being like gusts of wind. Each gust has a very small effect, pushing the child only slightly in a certain direction, but over time, if the wind is constant, large effects can be seen. Understanding how children learn from their environment is extremely useful in deciding how to avoid serious problems, and reduce conflict when it occurs.

Accidental rewards for misbehaviour

Teenagers can sometimes get what they want by behaving in ways that parents don't like. Problem behaviour is likely to keep occurring if it results in accidental rewards. Sometimes parents may not realise this is happening. For example, if you accidentally laugh or spend a lot of time reasoning with your teenager the first time they say a swear word, the extra attention may encourage your teenager to swear again. A teenager may discover that if they complain of feeling unwell, they get a lot of sympathetic attention and can perhaps also avoid doing unpleasant activities, such as homework. A gradual increase in complaining about feeling unwell may be the result. Accidental rewards can include social attention (such as talking or laughing), material rewards (such as money or things they want), activities (such as being driven somewhere or having a friend over), or avoiding chores (such as getting out of doing homework or washing the dishes).

> Do any of these accidental rewards occur in your family?
> - social attention ☐
> - material rewards ☑
> - activity rewards ☐
> - avoiding chores ☐
>
> Comments:
>
> when he goes out and we call him, and he does not answer the phone we stop the service than he does his best and behaves very good for just to get it back. then, as soon as we give it back he does the same thing he does not answer

Escalation traps

Teenagers may learn that 'turning up' or escalating undesirable behaviour is effective in getting what they want when their first request is turned down. For example, a teenager who wants to stay up late and watch a particular movie on TV may gradually become more aggressive, and complain loudly and emotionally of your unfair behaviour. After several minutes of this, you may give in and allow them to watch the movie. The persistent and escalating attack by the teenager is rewarded by getting what they want. This increases the chances that such demands will happen again in similar circumstances. In addition, your giving in is also rewarded by your teenager stopping the attack. This increases the chances that you will give in sooner next time.

Parents can also learn that if they escalate and get louder when they want their teenager to do something, their teenager is more likely to eventually comply with their requests. For example, you make a request for the TV to be turned off — your teenager ignores you! You repeat the request more loudly — still no result. Finally, you angrily demand that the TV be turned off before you count to 3 — or else! Your teenager finally complies, having learned that they only have to take notice of you when you count and threaten. Your escalating yelling and threatening is rewarded by the TV eventually being turned off, and this increases the chances you will have to yell and threaten more in the future. The teenager's delaying tactics are also rewarded by getting to watch a bit more TV, and then avoiding the threatened consequences by complying just before you explode. If this pattern of behaviour has been a feature of your family for some time, it may now be quite serious, with loud disputes between you and your teenager. As children grow older, they push the limits more. As they become bigger, stronger, and more verbally skilled, louder and longer fights are likely. In some families, parents become worn down by such persistent behaviour and end up giving in without a fight.

Which of these escalation traps occur in your family?

- teenager escalates ☑
- parent escalates ☐

Comments:

Staying the whole night in the computer and if I turn it off. He will scream and tell me I will not do the homework. then I stop to put the password to luck it.

he knows for the homework I do everything he asks.

✗ sleeping during the day and watching Tv.

✗ night time stiying in the computer.

Ignoring desirable behaviour

For some teenagers there is little or no payoff for good behaviour. Behaviour that earns no attention is likely to happen less often and even may stop altogether. If teenagers are ignored when they behave well, they may learn that the only way to get attention is to misbehave. As children grow older, they also learn that other people will give them attention — their peers. Sometimes behaviour that parents find desirable will be increased by peers (such as improving at sport), but often peer approval will increase behaviour that parents do not find desirable (such as body piercing).

HW

> Do you often fall into this trap?
>
> ● ignoring desirable behaviour ☐
>
> Comments:
>
> *I try when he does something good I tell him (beautifull) (thanks) I love it*

Watching others

Teenagers learn a lot by watching what other people do. For example, when parents get angry and yell at others, and get their own way because they yell, teenagers learn that it is ok to yell when they have a problem. Teenagers whose parents often hit them are likely to hit a lot as well. Behaviours such as yelling, talking back, losing your temper, swearing, hitting, and how to react when something frightening happens, can all be learned through watching others. Teenagers may also directly challenge parents who ask for a change of behaviour, stating *You do it, why shouldn't I?*

HW

> Does your teenager pick up any bad habits from watching others?
>
> ● parents? ☐
>
> ● siblings? ☐
>
> *Friends ——>*
> Comments:
>
> *big problem*
>
> *the key of problems*

Making requests

The way that parents attempt to get their teenagers to do things can influence whether or not they will cooperate. With younger children, parents often feel responsible for getting them to do things, like brush their teeth, eat their breakfast, wash their hands. However, older children and teenagers should be taking on these responsibilities without parents having to nag them constantly. Some common problems include:

- *Not enough information.* Teenagers sometimes seem disobedient because no-one has given them sufficient information about what is expected. Unless discussed previously, the request *Clean your room* does not specify what exactly it is that needs to be done. Does it mean — Sweep the floor? Pick up the clothes? Make the bed? Wash the windows? Or all of the above?

- *Poorly timed.* Requests made when a teenager is busy doing something else are likely to be not heard or ignored. Most of us don't like to be interrupted when we are busy and teenagers are no different.

- *Too vague.* Teenagers are unlikely (or unable) to follow requests that are unclear, such as *Stop that!* or *Don't be stupid!* Requests that appear optional and do not suggest a parent expects cooperation are also likely to be turned down, such as *Would you like to do your homework now?*

HW

How do you make requests?

- not enough information ☐
- poorly timed ☑
- too vague ☐

Comments:

Text in phone, face book, doing home work
watching tv . all the time their is
something their, or (tired)
        Later !

Emotional messages

Parents who disapprove of their teenager rather than their teenager's behaviour may lower their teenager's self esteem. Calling a teenager names — *stupid* or *idiot* — and guilt-inducing messages — *Your mother will be so upset when she hears about this* — may shame teenagers into cooperating. However, this can make teenagers angry, resentful and uncooperative.

Do you give any of these emotional messages?

- name calling or put downs ☑
- guilt inducing messages ☑

Comments:

when he does not listen I call him Selfesh, when he does thing are not apropret I call him dom

---

Ineffective use of punishment

Teenagers can develop behaviour problems because of the way parents use punishment or discipline. Here are some reasons why punishment does not work.

- *Punishment threatened but not carried out.* Threats may work for a while, but teenagers soon learn they can ignore them when parents don't follow through. Sometimes teenagers will treat a threat as a dare and will test it to see what happens. Teenagers who have learned over the years that parents rarely carry through with their threats will call their bluff regularly.

- *Punishment given in anger.* With young children, there is always a risk of losing control and injuring the child. With older children and teenagers, everyone can get injured, sometimes seriously.

- *Delayed punishment.* Sometimes parents overreact to problem behaviour because they wait until the behaviour is intolerable before doing something about it. With teenagers, this will often result in everyone yelling and losing their temper, and then not speaking to each other for days afterwards.

- *Inconsistent use of punishment.* Inconsistency makes it difficult for teenagers to learn what is expected of them. Punishing a behaviour on one occasion, and ignoring it the next time sends a confusing message. Problems can also arise when parents contradict or undermine each other, or do not back each other up. Teenagers will learn which parent to approach for particular requests, and this can cause relationship problems between parents.

Do you have any of these difficulties with discipline?

- punishment not carried out ☑
- punishment given in anger ☑
- delayed punishment ☐
- inconsistent use of punishment ☑

Comments:

Punishment ~~leads us~~ Lead to is ~~the~~ worst when we take his phone, he gets very angry, sometimes do not speak to each other for 1 or 2 days

HW

Parents' beliefs and expectations

Some beliefs are unhelpful and can make parenting difficult. Here are some common unhelpful beliefs.

- *It's just a phase.* This belief can stop parents from dealing with problem behaviour straight away. Instead, parents may wait until a problem is severe and long standing before seeking help or making changes.

- *They ought to know better.* Wishful thinking about how teenagers 'ought' to behave rarely results in improvement. Maybe the rules are not clear or perhaps there are other consequences that might be competing with parental approval.

- *They're doing it deliberately, just to annoy me.* This belief places blame on the teenager and may make parents resentful, leading them to over react to misbehaviour. It may also stop parents from looking at how their own actions contribute to the problem behaviour.

- *It's all my fault they're the way they are.* This belief blames parents for teenagers' problem behaviour. Parents may feel guilty and depressed if they think they are to blame for their teenager's behaviour. This makes it even harder to be patient, calm and consistent with their teenager.

Parents' expectations can also make parenting more difficult. It is unrealistic for parents to expect their teenager to be perfect. This is likely to lead to disappointment and conflict with their teenager. Parents can also have unrealistic expectations of themselves. When parents aim to do a perfect job, they are setting themselves up for dissatisfaction and frustration.

Do any of these apply to you?

- unhelpful beliefs ☐
- unrealistic expectations ☑

Comments:

when I ask them, or him to do something and they do not do it as I like, or supose to be done I get angry and they do too.

Other influences on the family

There are other influences on parents' wellbeing that can make parenting more difficult. Here are some examples:

- *Parents' relationship.* Problem behaviour can occur when a couple's relationship is strained and there is tension and conflict in the home. Boys may become aggressive and girls may become anxious or depressed when they see a lot of arguments and fights between their parents.

- *Parents' emotions.* Parents' feelings, such as anger, depression or anxiety, can prevent them from being consistent and managing their teenager's behaviour effectively. For example, if a parent is feeling sad or depressed, they are likely to be irritable and impatient, have unhelpful thoughts about their teenager, want to spend less time with their teenager, and provide less supervision.

- *Stress.* All parents experience stress at some time, such as moving house, financial problems, and work pressures. Teenagers need routine and may become upset if these stresses disrupt the usual family routine for a long period of time.

Do any of these apply to your family?

- parents' relationship with each other ☐
- parents' feelings ☑
- stress ☐

Comments:

when my child does something bad I feel sad, stressed, and angry, that day I feel I do not want to do anything even I do not pay attention to him

Influences Outside the Home

Teenagers' behaviour is also influenced by factors outside the home, once they have more contact with others in the community.

Peers and friends

As teenagers mix more with other teenagers at school and in social groups, they will be influenced by their relationships with these peers. For example, aggressive and disruptive children are often rejected by many of their peers, and fail to develop good social skills. They are then likely to mix with and learn from other disruptive teenagers. If this trend continues into the teenage years, it is likely that this will disrupt their schooling, and possibly bring them into contact with police and juvenile authorities.

School

Experiences at school can influence teenagers' adjustment and behaviour. For example if early problems are not identified and addressed, this may lead to academic failure, dislike of school, early dropout, and poor job prospects.

Media and technology

The influence of the media and computer technologies is a major factor for many teenagers. It is almost impossible for parents to control all access to movies, magazines, radio, TV, computer games, and web-sites. Problem behaviour such as swearing, fighting, smoking, drinking, and engaging in inappropriate sexual activity can be learned from these sources.

Which of these community influences on your teenager's behaviour are you concerned about?

- peers and friends ☑
- school ☐
- media and technology ☑

Comments:

I am tired of being with wrong people he loves to be, or copy his friends. pretending he is doing the home work, but he stays until 3 or 4 o'clock in the morning using the computer, or his phone text massaging or face book. it is very hard for me to control that.

Goals for Change

Now that you have looked at the possible factors influencing teenagers' behaviour, think about changes you would like to see in your teenager's behaviour, as well as in your own. It is up to you, the parent, to decide what skills to teach your teenager. It may be helpful to have in mind the skills that help teenagers learn to be independent and to get along with others.

EXERCISE 6 *What skills should we encourage in teenagers?*

Look at the list below and think about skills you would like to encourage in your teenager. Pick two or three to work on in Exercise 7.

How to communicate and get on with others

- Expressing their views, ideas and needs appropriately
- Requesting assistance or help when they need it
- Cooperating with adult requests
- Interacting cooperatively with others in an age-appropriate way
- Being aware of the feelings of others
- Being aware of how their own actions affect others

How to manage their feelings

- Expressing feelings in ways that do not harm others
- Controlling hurtful actions and thinking before acting
- Developing positive feelings about themselves and others
- Accepting rules and limits

How to be independent

- Doing things for themselves
- Completing tasks without constant adult supervision
- Being responsible for their own actions

How to solve problems

- Showing an interest in everyday things
- Asking questions and developing ideas
- Considering alternative solutions to problems
- Negotiating and compromising
- Making decisions and accepting the consequences of those decisions

Comments:

....

EXERCISE 7 *Setting goals for change*

When developing your goals for change, consider your teenager's behaviour now. Think of what you would like your teenager to do more often (e.g. speak politely, complete chores without constant adult reminding, cooperate with your requests, let you know where they are). Also consider what you would like your teenager to do less often (e.g. argue, fight, complain, interrupt, take things without asking). Write these goals for your teenager in the left hand column. It is also important to consider what changes you would like to make in your own behaviour. Now that you have looked at what may contribute to your teenager's problem behaviour, set yourself some goals. Consider what you would like to do more often (e.g. stay calm, make clear requests) and what you would like to do less often (e.g. use threats, shout instructions from a distance). Write these goals for your own behaviour in the right-hand column.

In the space below, list those changes that you would like to see in your teenager's behaviour and your own behaviour. Make sure your goals are specific and achievable and worded positively if possible.

GOALS FOR CHANGE IN YOUR TEENAGER'S BEHAVIOUR	GOALS FOR CHANGE IN YOUR OWN BEHAVIOUR
trust!	
being himself, stop copying other	be more close to my child (relationship)
Stop yelling and throwing things	stop yelling and over reacting
stoping being a kid accepting yes and no situations	stop worry about the kids
do well at school	

Keeping Track of Teenagers' Behaviour

EXERCISE 8 *Keeping track*

Behaviour diary

If you are concerned about some aspect of your teenager's behaviour, it is useful to keep track by keeping a behaviour diary. This involves writing down when and where a problem behaviour occurred, what happened before the problem behaviour (what led up to it) and what happened afterwards (how you reacted). This will help you to identify:

- how often the behaviour occurs
- patterns in your teenager's behaviour
- how consistently you deal with your teenager's behaviour
- high-risk times or situations
- possible triggers or causes
- possible accidental rewards.

An example behaviour diary for one day is shown below.

EXAMPLE BEHAVIOUR DIARY

Instructions: List the problem behaviour, when and where it occurred and what happened before and after the event.

Problem Behaviour: Peter's angry yelling   Day: Friday

PROBLEM EVENT	WHEN AND WHERE DID IT OCCUR?	WHAT OCCURRED BEFORE THE EVENT?	WHAT OCCURRED AFTER THE EVENT?	OTHER COMMENTS
Shouting at sister	7.30 a.m. Near bathroom	Sister using bathroom	Sister shouted back, dad sorted it out	Rushing to get ready for school
Angry at mother	8.00 a.m. Kitchen	Packing lunch in school bag	Got extra money for snacks	Didn't like lunch mother provided
Yelling at mother	4.00 p.m. Family room	Told to do homework before going out to see friends	Went out to see friends anyway	Couldn't be bothered arguing with him
Angry at sister	6.00 p.m. Kitchen	Sister using sink to wash dishes	Pushed in to get drink of water from tap	Too tired to interfere
Angry at father	7.30 p.m. Family room	Father came home without magazine	Peter and father yelled at each other Peter sent to his room	Father had promised to buy magazine for Peter and forgot

Tally sheet

When problem behaviours happen quite often, use a behaviour diary for a few occurrences, and then switch to another way to keep track of how often they occur. To do this, use a tally sheet like the one below, and mark off each time the behaviour occurs during the day. This is useful as an ongoing record of whether a behaviour is increasing or decreasing over time. It's important to start keeping track before you try and make any changes. This way you can tell if your new plan is working or not.

EXAMPLE TALLY SHEET

Instructions: Write the day in the first column, then place a tick in each successive square each time the problem behaviour occurs on that day. Record the total number of episodes for each day in the end column.

Behaviour: Swearing

Starting Date: Sunday May 11th

DAY	1	2	3	4	5	6	7	8	9	10	11	12	13	14	15	TOTAL
Sun	✓	✓	✓	✓	✓	✓	✓	✓	✓							9
Mon	✓	✓	✓	✓	✓	✓	✓	✓	✓	✓	✓					11
Tues	✓	✓	✓	✓	✓	✓	✓	✓								8

Duration record

Sometimes the number of times a behaviour occurs is not the crucial issue. It may be more important to note the duration of a behaviour. The duration record is a useful form for tracking how long a behaviour lasts, such as how long a teenager spends on the telephone, getting ready for school in the morning, or completing homework. The aim is to time how long each instance of the target behaviour lasts in minutes or hours, and write this on the chart. There may be only one instance of the behaviour per day, or there may be several. If there are several instances, at the end of the day, all episodes are added together to see the total amount of time the behaviour lasted for that day.

EXAMPLE DURATION RECORD

Instructions: Write the day in the first column, then for each separate occurrence of the target behaviour, record how long it lasted in seconds, minutes or hours. Total the times at the end of each day.

Behaviour: Time spent reading   Starting Date: March 20th

DAY	SUCCESSIVE EPISODES										TOTAL
	1	2	3	4	5	6	7	8	9	10	
Tues	5 min	15 min	10 min								30 min
Wed	10 min	10 min	5 min	5 min	20 min						50 min
Thurs	15 min	5 min									20 min

Time-sampling record

When problem behaviours happen too often or are difficult to count accurately, use a time-sampling record during parts of the day when the problem is occurring. To do this, use a record sheet like the one below. Divide the time into blocks of 15- or 30-minutes, and simply put a tick in the box if the problem behaviour occurs at all during that time. There is no need to count how many times the behaviour occurs, just tick if it occurs at all in each time interval.

EXAMPLE TIME-SAMPLING RECORD

Instructions: Place a tick in the square for the corresponding time period if the target behaviour has occurred at least once.

Behaviour: Arguing or talking back   Starting Date: March 20th

DAYS	M	T	W	T	F	S	S	M	T	W	T	F	S	S	M	T	W	T	F	S	S
8.00–8.15	✔			✔	✔																
8.15–8.30		✔	✔																		
8.30–8.45	✔	✔	✔																		
8.45–9.00					✔																
3.30–3.45		✔	✔				✔														
3.45–4.00	✔		✔																		
4.00–4.15	✔	✔	✔																		
4.15–4.30			✔		✔																
6.00–6.15	✔		✔	✔																	
6.15–6.30	✔		✔																		
6.30–6.45	✔	✔			✔																
6.45–7.00		✔			✔																
TOTAL	7	6	8	2	5	0	1														

TIME OF DAY

Behaviour graph

You can also put the information on a graph to make it easier to keep track of your teenager's progress (see below). Keep track like this for a week or so before you start any new parenting plan. Then, continue to keep track of your teenager's behaviour after you start, to see whether your new plan is successful. This will help you notice improvements in your teenager's behaviour and keep you motivated to continue using new strategies or routines.

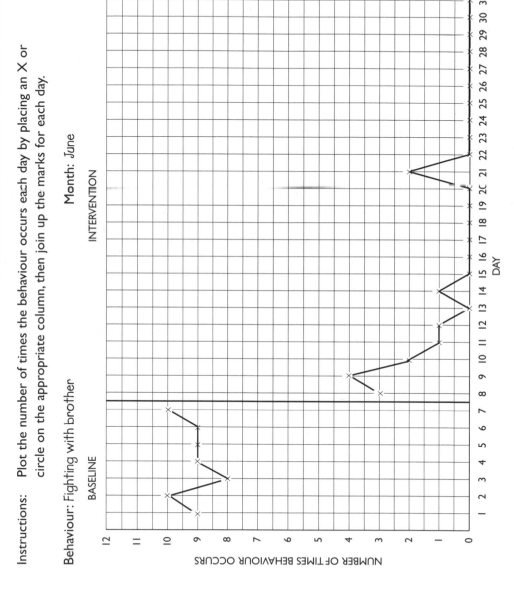

EXAMPLE BEHAVIOUR GRAPH

Instructions: Plot the number of times the behaviour occurs each day by placing an X or circle on the appropriate column, then join up the marks for each day.

Behaviour: Fighting with brother   Month: June

When you start a new parenting plan, it is useful to have a trial period of around 7 to 10 days. At the end of the trial period, you can decide whether to keep going in the same way or make minor changes to your plan. Remember, the best way to change teenagers' behaviour, and your own, is to do it gradually. Once new routines or behaviours are well established you can keep track less often, such as once a week instead of daily. Stop recording completely when you are confident of your progress. If you are concerned about your progress, talk to your group leader.

CONCLUSION

Summary of Session

Today's session has looked at what positive parenting involves and some factors influencing teenagers' behaviour. You have thought about the skills and behaviours you would like to encourage in your teenager and set some goals for change. To finish, you have looked at some ways of keeping track of your teenager's behaviour.

■ TASKS TO BE COMPLETED BETWEEN SESSIONS

- Use your list on page 15 to select one or two of your teenager's problem behaviours for baseline monitoring. Keep track of these behaviours for 7 days using a monitoring form from pages 23–27 in your workbook. Additional copies of these forms can be found in the Worksheets section at the back.

- Write down the behaviour/s you plan to track for the next 7 days. Which type of monitoring form will you use?

....

....

....

....

- Complete any unfinished exercises from today's session.

For a review of the material covered in today's session, you may like to read:

- Session 1 of *Teen Triple P Group Workbook*

or watch:

- *Every Parent's Guide to Teenagers*, Part 1, Positive Parenting
- *Every Parent's Guide to Teenagers*, Part 2, Factors Influencing Teenagers' Behaviour, Goals for Change, Keeping Track.

Content of Next Session

Session 2 will look at practical strategies for:

- building positive relationships with teenagers
- encouraging desirable behaviour
- teaching teenagers new skills and behaviours.

BEHAVIOUR DIARY

Instructions: List the problem behaviour, when and where it occurred and what happened before and after the event.

Problem Behaviour: _____

Day: _____

PROBLEM EVENT	WHEN AND WHERE DID IT OCCUR?	WHAT OCCURRED BEFORE THE EVENT?	WHAT OCCURRED AFTER THE EVENT?	OTHER COMMENTS

■ **TASK 1B** (complete between sessions)

TALLY SHEET

Instructions: Write the day in the first column, then place a tick in each successive square each time the behaviour occurs on that day. Record the total number of episodes for each day in the end column.

Behaviour: _____

Starting Date: _____

DAY	1	2	3	4	5	6	7	8	9	10	11	12	13	14	15	TOTAL

DURATION RECORD

Instructions: Write the day in the first column, then for each separate occurrence of the target behaviour, record how long it lasted in seconds, minutes or hours. Total the times at the end of each day.

Behaviour: _____   Starting Date: _____

DAY	SUCCESSIVE EPISODES										TOTAL
	1	2	3	4	5	6	7	8	9	10	

■ **TASK 1D** (complete between sessions)

TIME-SAMPLING RECORD

Instructions: Place a tick in the square for the corresponding time period if the target behaviour has occurred at least once.

Behaviour: ______________________________ Starting Date: ______________

TIME OF DAY

DAYS	M	T	W	T	F	S	S	M	T	W	T	F	S	S	M	T	W	T	F	S	S
TOTAL																					

BEHAVIOUR GRAPH

Instructions: Plot the number of times the behaviour occurs each day by placing an X or circle in the appropriate column, then join up the marks for each day.

Behaviour:

Month:

BASELINE   INTERVENTION

NUMBER OF TIMES BEHAVIOUR OCCURS

DAY

0 1 2 3 4 5 6 7 8 9 10 11 12 13 14 15 16 17 18 19 20 21 22 23 24 25 26 27 28 29 30 31

Encouraging Appropriate Behaviour

Session 2

OVERVIEW

Encouragement and positive attention help teenagers develop their skills and learn appropriate ways of behaving. Encouraging the behaviour you like increases the chances of the behaviour happening again. In Session 1, you decided on some of the behaviours and skills you would like to encourage in your teenager. In this session, you will be introduced to a number of strategies to try out. These strategies can help you encourage your teenager to behave appropriately by enhancing your relationship with your teenager, rewarding your teenager for desirable behaviour, and teaching your teenager new skills. As you work through today's exercises, think about the strategies you would feel most comfortable using with your teenager.

OBJECTIVES

By the end of Session 2, you should be able to:

- use the strategies for developing a positive relationship with your teenager (i.e. spending time together, talking to teenager, showing affection)
- use the strategies for encouraging desirable behaviour (i.e. descriptive praise, providing attention, and providing opportunities for engaging activities for your teenager)
- use the strategies for teaching teenager new skills or behaviours (i.e. setting a good example, coaching problem solving)
- choose two positive parenting strategies to practise and monitor for 7 days
- set up a behaviour contract with appropriate rewards for your teenager.

Session 2

Developing Positive Relationships With Teenagers

It takes time to form quality family relationships that last. Here are some ideas to help you develop a positive relationship with your teenager.

Spend time with your teenager

Spending frequent, small amounts of time with teenagers can be just as beneficial as less frequent longer periods. However, there will be times when longer periods are needed. Try and work out when are good times for your teenager. These can be when you are alone together, and when there is no pressure to get things done, such as driving in the car together, at bedtime, or on weekends.

EXERCISE 1 *Ideas on how to spend time with your teenager*

> Write down some ideas about how you and your teenager can spend time together.
>
> *Spend time with them, talk to them, show them care, affection*

Talk with your teenager

Sometimes when you are spending time together there will be an opportunity to talk. A good way to start is with something about yourself — what happened during your day perhaps — or ask about something you know they are interested in. This might include things you have done together, or are about to do. Make sure you listen to the things your teenager talks about and show interest. Try not to slip into teaching or interrogation mode — practise asking clarifying questions, reflect what you hear them say, and occasionally offer items from your own experience. Be prepared to talk for longer if they start to talk about issues or problems. If there is not enough time, arrange another time as soon as you can and keep to it.

EXERCISE 2 *Things to talk about*

> List some things that interest your teenager or that you have been doing that you can talk about.
>
> _ music
> _driving
> _ work to get stress / working to loss wight

Show affection

One of the best ways to maintain a good relationship with your teenager is to show them you care about them. This needs to be done differently from when they were younger, as public displays of affection may cause embarrassment — especially in front of their peers. Affection should be displayed more in keeping with adult relationships. It is important to show teenagers how to appropriately give and receive affection as an adult.

EXERCISE 3 *Ways to show affection*

> What ways of showing affection do you and your teenager enjoy?
>
> hug the child tell him I love you

Increasing Desirable Behaviour

Rewarding behaviour you like increases the chance of that behaviour happening again. Here are some ideas you can use to increase your teenager's appropriate behaviour.

Praise your teenager

Everyone likes to receive praise, even though some teenagers (and adults) may pretend they do not. Notice what your teenager does, without making it too obvious, and praise the behaviour you like. With teenagers, it needs to be more subtle than with younger children. Just a few words may be enough, such as *Thanks for keeping the music down while I was on the phone* or *You did a great job of cleaning the car.* But make sure you describe exactly what it was that you liked, as this is more effective than just a general *Thanks* or *Well done*. Praise works best when you are enthusiastic and mean what you say.

EXERCISE 4 *How to give descriptive praise*

> Look at your list of goals for things you would like your teenager to do more often (see page 15 of this workbook). In the space below, write down two of these behaviours and the descriptive praise you could use to encourage these behaviours. Try to be as specific and descriptive as you can.
>
> Behaviour: Vacum
>
> Descriptive praise: Thank you for doing vacuming You can't imagine how it helps me
>
> Behaviour:
>
> Descriptive praise: I like

Give your teenager attention

There are many ways of giving attention. A smile, wink, pat on the back or just watching are all forms of attention that teenagers enjoy and can be used to encourage behaviour you like. These actions add to your praise and show your teenager how pleased you are with their behaviour. You can also use these forms of attention to encourage your teenager for behaving well in situations where you are unable to praise them, such as when they are in a group of friends and your praise may embarrass them. Remember, you can give attention *specifically* to increase a desirable behaviour, and *generally to* promote a positive relationship.

EXERCISE 5 *Ways to give attention*

> Write down some ways you can give attention to your teenager.
> Smile, listen, support what they like
> exe
> I like how you dress today

Provide opportunities for engaging activities

Not every parent can afford to buy the latest in computer games, music players, and other expensive equipment. However, it is still important to provide teenagers with opportunities to explore a range of interesting things to do. The local library, community newspaper, and recreation centres often provide information about many opportunities to experience new activities at low cost. You may need to go along for the first few times to help your teenager feel comfortable, or you may decide to do something together, or as a family.

EXERCISE 6 *Ideas for engaging activities*

Think of some fun new activities for your teenager. You may like to get some ideas from other parents. List some activities for indoors and outdoors.

INDOOR ACTIVITIES	OUTDOOR ACTIVITIES
listen to music with him	go to Gym as Vistor guest
I need to lose fat in my stonck help or show me	driving together

Teaching New Skills and Behaviours

Set a good example

We all learn through watching others. To encourage new behaviours, let your teenager watch you. Describe what you are doing and let your teenager copy your actions. Provide help if necessary and encourage your teenager to try again without any help. Praise your teenager when they are successful.

Do not expect your teenager to behave appropriately if no one else in the family does. For example, you cannot expect your teenager to tidy away after themselves if you leave your own things lying around. Set a good example to show your teenager how to behave.

EXERCISE 7 *Ways to set a good example*

> From your list of goals for your teenager's behaviour (on page 15 of your workbook), decide if there are any behaviours you can encourage by setting a good example. List them below.
>
> *Set a good example*
> *teach them how to do things*

Coach problem solving

This is something that can be used when your teenager asks for information, or when they are struggling with a problem. At these times they are often motivated to learn. With younger children, parents usually know or can work out an answer, but with teenagers it may be something neither of you knows the answer to. Even if you do have an answer, try not to give it right away, as this does not help your teenager learn to think for themselves.

With a **clear-cut problem**, prompt your teenager to come up with the answer, or a way of finding out how to get the answer: *What do* **you** *think?* or *How do you think we could find out?* This should be something you can do together. Ensure your teenager does whatever they can to find the answer, but help where you can, and give the answer if they cannot come up with it. There will be lots of opportunities for this type of learning exchange, especially if you are helpful.

EXERCISE 8 *How to coach problem solving*

> There are different types of teaching opportunities that occur frequently. Think of how you could coach your teenager to problem solve in the following situations:
>
> When your teenager asks you questions, particularly the common *How?* or *Why?* questions (e.g. *How can I find out what time the next train/bus goes to town?*).
>
> *help then to get soluation guid them*
>
> *give Allowness to you Teen*
>
> *How do you think t*
> *ask Question ? How they fint sol4ution*

do not give answer

When your teenager cannot think of the right word for something
(e.g. *What's another way of saying someone is rude?*).

When your teenager is frustrated with an activity and asks for help
(e.g. *I can't work out how to do this!*).

- *did you read instructer ?*
- *what did not work about it*
- *why do not try*

If the problem is **more complex** and there is no clear solution, more time will be needed and you may find it helpful to go through the steps below.

Goal

Help your teenager to clarify the problem, and agree on what the goal is. What will the situation be like when the problem has been solved?

Options

There are usually a number of ways a goal can be reached and the first one thought of is not always the best. Consider a range of options before deciding which one has the best chance of achieving the goal. Together, think of as many possible solutions as you can.

Consequences

Before deciding which option to try, first check to see what the likely consequences will be for each option. Sometimes an option will achieve the goal, but have undesirable side-effects that can be noted in advance with a bit of thought. Decide on the best option. Sometimes combining two options brings the best results.

Trial it

When the best option has been selected, work out how to give it every chance of working and then give it a try. It is sometimes best to have a second option ready (Plan B) in case the first does not work as planned.

Review

Whether it works or not, it is always a good idea to review what happened. This can be an opportunity to congratulate each other on a good plan, or to try again. Either way it is important to praise cooperation and success. Also, a review can be a good learning experience for the next time a problem comes up.

giving away your power

Think of a recent problem that requires more than a single prompt to find a solution. In pairs, decide how best to work through the problem. Use the space below to note down how you go. You won't be able to complete the final review step unless you actually try out your selected solution.

Problem: ....

GOAL	
OPTIONS	
CONSEQUENCES	
PLAN FOR TRIAL	
REVIEW	

Remember that your job as parent is not to solve the problem yourself, but to raise important questions, and to make suggestions only when necessary. Your teenager will not learn much about solving problems if you do all the work every time!

Use a behaviour contract

When a new behaviour is being learned, you may find it necessary to provide extra motivation until it is firmly established. With teenagers, this can take some weeks and a degree of persistence on your part! A behaviour contract can be very useful here. It is an effective short-to-medium term strategy that can be used for a while and then phased out. Your teenager can earn privileges in return for improvements in the desired behaviour. This gives them a sense of achievement and recognition for their efforts. It is most important that the contract be negotiated with your teenager, even though they may not end up fully agreeing with it.

Some parents object to the idea of providing rewards for behaviour that they believe teenagers should just do. The problem is that if the behaviours parents want are not occurring, despite their best efforts at persuasion, the only other options are to use aggressive standover tactics, or nag and yell at the teenager until they do what the parent wants. In the longer term, these tactics cause resentment and anger all round, and often lead to serious conflict. Alternatively, parents can just give in and do it themselves. However, the teenager then avoids learning the skills they will need when they leave home to live as an independent adult.

EXERCISE 9 *Using a behaviour contract*

Select one or two behaviours you would like to see your teenager do, or do more of, that you do not think other strategies will work for. For many parents this may be a family chore. You may find it helpful to go through the Family Jobs List on the next page and review who currently does the chores in your family, and whether your teenager currently benefits from the efforts of others while doing very little themselves.

Write down tasks from the Family Jobs List (or others) you want your adolescent to take more responsibility for doing.

- computer time   / time limits

- Reward improvement

family meeting is very important
(group discation

FAMILY JOBS LIST

On the left, next to each activity or chore, write the names of the family member/s who currently do or help with each task. On the right of each activity or chore, write the names of any other family member who benefits from it being done. For example, a parent might make everyone's breakfast, so their name goes on the left, and everyone else's name goes on the right. Complete this for all the activities on the list that apply to your family.

Who currently does the chore?	Activity/chore	Who benefits?
....	Making breakfast	....
....	Making lunch	....
....	Making evening meal	....
....	Shopping for food	....
....	Fixing things that are broken	....
....	Washing the dishes	....
....	Washing clothes	....
....	Ironing clothes	....
....	Mending clothes	....
....	Sweeping/vacuuming	....
....	Putting out garbage	....
....	Cleaning house	....
....	Feeding pets	....
....	Looking after/ exercising pets	....
....	Mowing the lawn	....
....	Weeding the garden	....
....	Cleaning the bath/ shower	....
....	Cleaning the windows	....
....	Cleaning/washing the car	....
....	Any other chores (specify)	....
....	....	....
....	....	....
....	....	....

Next, think of what your teenager can receive for improving or increasing the desired behaviour/s. You should discuss this with your teenager to get their ideas on things they would like to work for. Here are some suggestions:

Family activities

- Board games (chess, Monopoly™)
- Card games (500, rummy)
- Puzzles (jigsaws, charades)
- Social events (BBQ, picnic at beach, party)
- Eating out (burgers, pizza, seafood)

Other activities

- Watching TV
- Renting DVDs
- Computer games
- Reading, being read to
- Making things (model, something for their room)
- Travel, holidays
- Swimming, surfing, sailing, skating
- Having haircut/postponing haircut
- Going to library, art gallery, museum

Being with:

- Friends (at their home or yours)
- Parents (activity specified by teenager)
- Relatives (selected by teenager)
- Animals
- Others

Special edibles

- Ice cream, chocolate, cool drinks
- Favourite meals, desserts, cakes
- Special snacks, pizza

Special events

- Trips (zoo, wildlife park)
- Movies, shows
- Sporting event (football, basketball)
- Having friends stay over
- Sleeping over at friend's
- Shopping, camping out

Buying:

- Magazines, CDs, tapes
- Computer games
- Clothes, books
- A pet

Use of:

- Computer
- TV
- Telephone
- Bike, skateboard, roller blades
- Tools, sport equipment
- Parent's clothes/jewelry

Remember to choose rewards that you believe your teenager will enjoy.

Behaviour contract guidelines

Here are some guidelines for constructing a workable behaviour contract to encourage appropriate behaviour:

- Clearly describe the behaviour(s) that will be the focus of the contract. State the behaviour positively, such as *Wash the dishes after every evening meal* or *Feed the dog every morning before going to school.*

- Agree on what the rewards will be for improvements in the selected behaviour/s. It is best to match or link the reward to the behaviour. Chores completed around the home might earn the right to watch a favourite TV show, or buy a new magazine. Improvements in helpfulness or politeness might earn the right to choose a preferred take-away meal for Friday night, or select a DVD for the family to watch. Compliance with homework requirements or music practice might earn the right to go to a friend's party on the weekend. Some of the best rewards involve activities, such as special time with you, or a family visit to a special place.

- Agree on what level of behaviour will earn what level of reward. Do not expect new behaviours to be learned perfectly at first. Reward improvement over past levels, rather than aiming for instant perfection. If your teenager makes an extra effort, but then does not earn a reward, the motivation to keep trying will fade and no lasting change will occur. You can always make changes to the contract in later weeks to require them to improve more to earn the reward.

- If the behaviour is one that just has to occur, such as being ready on time to go to school, a backup penalty for not succeeding may be necessary. It is generally much better to rely on rewards to improve desirable behaviour, but sometimes it will be necessary to arrange a penalty for missing deadlines.

- Select rewards that are practical and within your budget. If your teenager wants a large reward (such as a new bike), spread it over several months. For example, get a picture of a bike and cut it up into, say, 20 pieces — then stick the picture together piece by piece as each piece is earned. This also allows you to save up over several months. However, small rewards given daily are much better than large rewards given weeks or months later. Sometimes it is appropriate to arrange both. The small rewards keep the new behaviour going on a daily basis, and the large reward keeps it going over a period of weeks. Also it is a good idea to have a range of rewards to choose from to prevent your teenager getting bored with just one. A reward can lose its effect over time if it is obtained too often or is too far off.

- Select rewards that you have control over. It is pointless to agree to extra TV or computer time if your teenager has their own TV or computer in their room to use whenever they like. Similarly, it is no use offering to pay them a small amount of money every time they mow the lawn if they have a part-time job and earn a much larger regular amount.

- Make sure that whatever reward you promise, you can deliver it. Nothing undermines a behaviour contract more than not getting the agreed reward. Imagine how you would feel if an employer did not pay as promised, or a friend cheated on a loan! If there is a possibility that this could happen, make sure you discuss this immediately and arrange a way of making it up.

The next step is to specify what behaviour will earn what reward. There are lots of different ways to organise this. Some are quite simple, and others are more complicated. Try and keep it simple to start with. There are two examples provided in the example contracts #1A and #1B on the next pages.

Link the behaviour you want to see more of with the reward you have agreed with your teenager. Remember to set moderately easy goals at first so your teenager is rewarded for their extra effort, then you can gradually make the goals harder to achieve.

....

....

....

....

Finally, list anything you need to purchase or organise before you can start using the contract.

....

....

....

....

Before putting a Behaviour Contract into effect there are two final steps. Write down the agreed contract details and prepare a monitoring chart to track progress through the week. Write down the agreement and get everyone to sign. It may seem unnecessary, but it saves a lot of argument later, when it may be hard to remember what was agreed.

There are two examples of Monitoring Charts on the next two pages and there is a blank Behaviour Contract form on page 44 to give you an idea what they look like.

If the new behaviour improves as promised, you must provide the agreed reward for the system to work. If another problem occurs do not punish your teenager by withholding the earned reward. Negotiate a separate new contract to deal with the new problem. You may get some ideas from the next section on Managing Problem Behaviour, which also recommends the use of behaviour contracts, but with some additional features.

Between: John   **and:** Mom

Starting on: Monday June 12th

Behaviour/chore:
John will make his bed and clean up his room before 7.30am on schooldays and before breakfast on non-school days.

Reward: Watch one hour of TV after school between 5pm and 6pm (or anytime on weekends and holidays).

Conditions: If jobs not completed on time, no TV permitted that day before 6pm.

EXAMPLE MONITORING CHART #1A

Name: John   **Week beginning:** Monday June 12th

ACTIVITY & DETAILS	CARRY OVER	M	TU	W	TH	F	SA	SU	TOTAL
Make bed, and clean up room, before breakfast daily	N/A								

EXAMPLE BEHAVIOUR CONTRACT #1B

Between: Jane   **and:** Dad

Starting on: Monday June 12th

Behaviour/chore:

Jane will clear away dishes after the evening meal, stack the dishwasher before 8pm, and feed the dog each day before breakfast.

Reward: Clearing away dishes = 3pts; Stacking dishwasher = 2 points; Feeding the dog = 1 point. Each point may be exchanged for 10 mins of telephone time.

Conditions: No credit allowed, but unused points may be carried over to the next day. Telephone calls may be made to a maximum of 60 minutes between 6pm and 9pm on school-days. No more than 1 hour of telephone time can be carried over to the following week.

EXAMPLE MONITORING CHART #1B

Name: Jane   **Week beginning:** Monday June 12th

ACTIVITY & DETAILS	CARRY OVER	M	TU	W	TH	F	SA	SU	TOTAL
Clear away dishes (3pts) Stack dishwasher (2pts) Feed dog (1pt)									
TOTAL EARNED PER DAY									
1pt = 10 mins phone time;									
Time earned									
Time used									
Time remaining									

BEHAVIOUR CONTRACT #1

Between: .... and: ....

Starting on: .... (date)

Behaviour/chore: ....

....

....

....

Reward: ....

....

....

....

Conditions: ....

....

....

....

MONITORING CHART #1

Name: .... Week beginning: ....

ACTIVITY & DETAILS	CARRY OVER	M	TU	W	TH	F	SA	SU	TOTAL

Family Meetings

Working out family problems and writing behaviour contracts can take a bit of time and cannot be done in a hurry. Many families often discover there are few occasions when they come together to discuss matters of importance, or simply to enjoy talking to each other. One way to address this is to organise a family meeting for an appropriate time during the week. This will give the message that you are serious about dealing with these matters, and increases the chances that they will be well done and will work. Family meetings do not need to be long and boring, although this may be the initial reaction to the idea, especially by teenagers. It is therefore important to make them brief, focused, and as enjoyable as possible. Here are some suggestions about planning and holding family meetings:

- If possible, pick a time when everyone can be present on a regular weekly basis, and keep to it. Select a time when people are not too tired, and not right after or before other commitments to avoid rushing. Sometimes you may need to change it, or accept that someone cannot make it, but aim for a regular meeting time.

- Pick a setting that is comfortable and away from other distractions (TV, radio). Each family member should be able to see everyone else. Around the dining table is a good place for many families.

- Take the meeting seriously and have a set agenda so that everyone knows what is going to be discussed, but allow people to bring other issues up as well (see the example agenda on page 49).

- Set time limits for meetings. Perhaps start with 15 minutes to get people used to the idea, and then increase the time gradually as needed. It is rarely a good idea to meet for as long as an hour unless there is a big problem to work on.

- Discourage visitors and phone calls during meeting times. Either switch the answering machine on, unplug the telephone, or tell people who phone that you will call back later. Remove or turn off other possible distractions such as TV and radio, although some peaceful background music may be suitable if everyone agrees.

- Agree on rules for the meeting. *If someone needs to leave the meeting, ask permission; Only one person at a time can speak; Speak quietly*, are some examples that you might wish to use.

- Stop the meeting if any one person makes more than three hostile comments or rule violations. Deal with the problem away from the meeting, and hold the meeting later, with or without the offending person. Always invite everyone, but do not force anyone to attend. If problem behaviour continues, make a note to include it for discussion at the next group session.

- It can be helpful to nominate different people for different jobs. A *chairperson* can make sure people keep to the agenda. A *recorder* can write down any decisions that are made. A *time-keeper* can make sure there is enough time to discuss every item, and a *mediator* can help people to keep to the rules. It is best to rotate these jobs so that everyone gets a chance in each job. That way everyone learns more and feels involved.

- If possible, arrange for a pleasant family activity to follow the family meeting, such as a family game, snack, or DVD.

- Family meetings can also be used to discuss the coming week, organize weekends and holidays, or deal with issues that keep getting put off. As family members experience benefits from sitting down to plan together, they may be more willing to participate.

EXERCISE 10 *Planning a family meeting*

Think about when you could hold a family meeting. You may like to call a family meeting to discuss the behaviour contract you are planning.

....

....

....

....

CONCLUSION

In today's session, 10 positive parenting strategies were introduced. These included:
- spending time with your teenager
- talking to your teenager
- showing affection
- praising your teenager
- giving your teenager attention
- providing opportunities for engaging activities
- setting a good example
- coaching problem solving
- using a behaviour contract
- holding a family meeting.

Think about which of these strategies you would like to use with your teenager.

■ TASKS TO BE COMPLETED BETWEEN SESSIONS

- Choose two strategies to try out with your teenager. Keep track of how you go by using the checklist on page 48 of your workbook. An additional copy of this form is provided in the Worksheets section.

- Write down the two strategies you plan to use over the next 7 days.

....

....

....

....

- Hold a family meeting (see the example agenda on page 49) to discuss the Family Jobs List (page 50) and redraft the behaviour contract you have begun to write (use the blank form on page 51). However, do not start using it with your teenager until after the next session which will provide more information.

- Continue monitoring the behaviours you selected at the end of Session1 (page 21 of your Workbook) and keep track of progress on the recording form and the Behaviour Graph.

- Complete any unfinished exercises from today's session.

For a review of the material covered in today's session, you may like to read:

- Session 2 of *Teen Triple P Group Workbook*

or watch:

- *Every Parent's Guide to Teenagers,* Part 3, Encouraging Appropriate Behaviour.

Content of Next Session

Session 3 will look at practical strategies for managing problem behaviour and helping teenagers to develop self-control.

CHECKLIST FOR ENCOURAGING APPROPRIATE BEHAVIOUR

Choose two of the strategies introduced in Session 2 that you would like to practise with your teenager over the next week. Be as specific as possible (e.g. one goal may be to use descriptive praise statements with your teenager at least three times per day). Use the table below to record whether you reached your goals each day. Comment on what went well and list any problems that occurred.

GOAL 1: ....

....

....

GOAL 2: ....

....

....

DAY	GOAL 1 Y/N	GOAL 2 Y/N	COMMENTS
1			
2			
3			
4			
5			
6			
7			

EXAMPLE AGENDA FOR FAMILY MEETING #1

Preparation

- Agree on time and place for meeting; agree on realistic time-limit (e.g. 30 minutes)
- Gather all relevant material together from noticeboard, etc
- Appoint *chairperson*, *timekeeper* and *recorder*, etc.

Agenda

- *Item 1*: Discuss Family Jobs List and new behaviours/chores for teenager
- *Item 2*: Discuss possible rewards that will be linked to new behaviours/chores
- *Item 3*: Negotiate *draft* Behaviour Contract #1 (do not implement)
- *Item 4*: Draw up Monitoring Chart
- *Item 5*: Any other business
- *Item 6*: Set time for next meeting

Before closing the meeting, quickly review any important decisions that have been made.

Afterwards

Where possible, organise some brief pleasant activity for all family members to do together to reward everyone for taking part in the family meeting.

FAMILY JOBS LIST

Who currently does the chore?	Activity/chore	Who benefits?
....	Making breakfast	....
....	Making lunch	....
....	Making evening meal	....
....	Shopping for food	....
....	Fixing things that are broken	....
....	Washing the dishes	....
....	Washing clothes	....
....	Ironing clothes	....
	Mending clothes	
....	Sweeping/vacuuming	....
....	Putting out garbage	....
....	Cleaning house	....
....	Feeding pets	....
....	Looking after/ exercising pets	....
....	Mowing the lawn	....
....	Weeding the garden	....
....	Cleaning the bath/ shower	....
....	Cleaning the windows	....
....	Cleaning/washing the car	....
	Any other chores (specify)	
....	....	....
....	....	....
....	....	....

Session 2

BEHAVIOUR CONTRACT #1

Between: .... and: ....

Starting on: .... (date)

Behaviour/chore: ....

....

....

....

Reward: ....

....

....

Conditions: ....

....

....

....

MONITORING CHART #1

Name: .... Week beginning: ....

ACTIVITY & DETAILS	CARRY OVER	M	TU	W	TH	F	SA	SU	TOTAL

Managing Problem Behaviour

All teenagers need to learn to accept limits and to control their disappointment when they do not get what they want. Managing these situations can be challenging for parents, particularly if this has been a problem during a teenager's younger years. However, there are positive and effective ways to help teenagers learn self-control, and defer short-term benefits in favour of longer-term goals. Teenagers learn self-control when their parents use consequences for problem behaviour *immediately*, *consistently* and *decisively*. Several options for managing teenagers' problem behaviour that parents may have to deal with at home will be presented in today's session. Consider each as an option you could use with your family. There will be lots of opportunities for you to practise these strategies to help you decide which ones you would like to use. In the final session, strategies for dealing with more risky behaviour that may occur outside the home will be introduced.

OBJECTIVES

By the end of Session 3, you should be able to:

- set appropriate family rules and discuss them with your family
- use directed discussion to deal with mild problem behaviour
- make clear, calm requests
- back up your requests with logical consequences
- deal calmly with emotional behaviour
- put into practice a behaviour contract to manage problem behaviour.

Managing Problem Behaviour

Establishing clear family rules

Teenagers need limits to know what is expected of them and how they should behave. A few basic family rules (no more than four or five) can help. Rules should tell teenagers what to do, rather than what not to do. *Walk in the house*, *Speak in a pleasant voice* and *Keep your hands and feet to yourself* are better rules than *Don't run*, *Don't shout* and *Don't fight*. Rules work best when they are fair, easy to follow, and you can back them up. Try to involve your teenager in deciding on family rules. The key points to remember are:

- have a small number of rules
- rules should be fair
- rules should be easy to follow
- rules should be enforceable
- rules should be positively stated.

Here are some rules that other parents have selected. They are all stated positively with the problem behaviour included in brackets as a guide.

EXAMPLE FAMILY RULES

- Be honest (not untruthful)
- Be polite (not rude)
- Be assertive (not aggressive or too passive)
- Be reliable (not unreliable)
- Be gentle (not rough)
- Be kind (not mean or hurtful)
- Be positive and constructive (not negative or destructive)

- Be helpful and considerate (not unhelpful or inconsiderate)
- Speak quietly (not yelling or shouting)
- Respect others' property and privacy (not taking things or going into rooms without asking)

EXERCISE **1** *Establishing clear rules*

In the space provided, list up to four or five rules that you would like to use in your home.

- few, fair,
don't do this, and ask then do not do it
- be clear about the rules

Use directed discussion to deal with rule breaking

Even when you have a set of family rules that everyone knows, your teenager may 'forget' and break the rule. Sometimes, especially when a new rule has just been agreed, you can use Directed Discussion to remind the teenager what he or she is meant to do. It involves gaining his or her attention, specifying the behaviour of concern, asking for the rule to be stated, and then requiring the correct behaviour. For example — *Joan, you are speaking too loudly. What's our rule about how to speak to each other? … OK, now let's start again and follow that rule.* And when they follow the rule, make sure you praise them — *Thank you for following the rule.*

If your teenager does not follow this request, you will need to back it up with a consequence (see pages 57–58 of your Workbook — this section will be covered later in the Session).

EXERCISE 2 *Using directed discussion to deal with rule breaking*

Think of a rule that occasionally gets broken in your house or imagine that your teenager has just broken one of your new rules. Write down *what you could say* to your teenager at each step of a directed discussion to teach your teenager the correct behaviour.

Situation:..

....

Gain your teenager's attention:..

....

State the problem briefly, simply and calmly: ....

....

Briefly explain why the behaviour is a problem: ....

....

Ask your teenager to suggest the correct behaviour:................

....

Request that your teenager practise the correct behaviour: ....

....

Praise your teenager for the correct behaviour: ....

....

- ask him about
what our rule?
- can please pick up your clothes.
- thank you.

Make clear, calm requests

As well as expecting teenagers to follow family rules, there will be occasions when parents want their teenager to cooperate with their requests. The way requests are made influences whether a teenager will cooperate or not — and whether or not parents have to deal with problem behaviour.

When making a request of a teenager it is important to be polite, clear, and specific. However, it is not reasonable to always insist on instant obedience. As children get older, give them more freedom to complete a required task when it suits them, within reason, although you should still set time limits. However, if a problem behaviour is occurring that you want to stop, act immediately. When you want your teenager to do something right away, be prepared to back up your request if it is not carried out. When you want your teenager to cooperate, follow these steps:

Get your timing right

No one likes being interrupted when they are involved in something important or enjoyable. Give advance notice where possible — *Please be ready to go out in 20 minutes.*

Get close and gain your teenager's attention

Stop what you are doing and move so they can easily see and hear you. Use their name to gain their attention.

Describe what you want your teenager to do

Be specific, and say exactly what you want them to do — *Peter, please turn off the TV at seven o'clock because I'm putting dinner on the table then.*

Give your teenager time to cooperate

Allow enough time for your teenager to do what you asked.

Praise cooperation

If your teenager cooperates with your request, praise them - *Thank you for turning the TV off and coming to the table as I asked Peter.*

Provide a back up consequence for non-cooperation

If your teenager does not cooperate, do not give a second chance. This may be appropriate with younger children, but older children should have learned to do what is asked at the first time of asking. Back up your request with a consequence. Never threaten to apply a consequence as this will teach your teenager only to respond to your requests when a threat is included. Threats also increase the emotional temperature and make an argument more likely. Suggestions about what consequences might be used, and how to apply them, are covered in Exercise 4 (pages 58 and 59).

EXERCISE 3 *Making clear, calm requests*

> Write down some examples of clear, calm requests you could use in the following situations:
>
> Your teenager's TV time allocation is used up but they continue to watch it.
>
> ....
>
> ....
>
> ....
>
> Your teenager is interrupting your telephone call by turning the TV up quite loud.
>
> ....
>
> ....
>
> ....
>
> Your teenager's wet towels and swimsuit are scattered on the floor.
>
> ....
>
> ....
>
> ....
>
> Your teenager is yelling at a younger sibling to return a radio they borrowed.
>
> ....
>
> ....
>
> ....
>
> Your teenager is eating a snack in front of the TV, and food scraps are being spilled on to the carpet.
>
> ....
>
> ....
>
> ....

thank them when they respond
15 to 30 ~~time~~ minutes

Back up your requests with logical consequences

Grounding teenagers for lengthy periods when they misbehave does not work well. First, it usually punishes you as well because you have to monitor the teenager closely to make the grounding work. Second, many parents give in before the time is over — the teenager then learns that you do not mean what you say. Third, taking away your teenager's freedom is a very powerful penalty. Once you do this, you cannot use it again until you give it back. And finally, it is important to give your teenager an opportunity to demonstrate they have learned to behave better.

Therefore, impose a short, but powerful consequence, and then allow the teenager the opportunity to show they have learned. If they have not, you can always impose the consequence again until they do.

Logical consequences are best used for behaviour problems that do not occur too often. If your teenager does not follow a clear request, choose a consequence that fits the situation if you can. If possible, remove the activity or equipment that is at the center of the problem. Logical consequences work best if they are brief — 15 to 30 minutes is usually long enough. When a problem occurs, follow these steps:

Withdraw the activity

Do not debate or argue the point. Act as soon as the problem occurs. Explain why you are removing access to the activity — *You are not sharing this computer game with your younger brother as agreed so I'm switching it off for 15 minutes*, or, *You haven't turned the volume down on the hi-fi as I asked, so I'm switching it off for 30 minutes.*

Return the activity

Remember to keep to the agreement. When the time is up, return the activity so your teenager can practise how to behave appropriately. Try to prevent the same thing happening again by coaching them on how to solve the problem.

Use another consequence if necessary

If a problem occurs again within the next hour or so after returning the activity, follow up by removing the activity for a longer period, such as the rest of the day. If the problem occurs regularly, consider writing a behaviour contract to deal with it. The section on using Behaviour Contracts to manage problem behaviour is covered later in this session — see page 65 in your workbook.

EXERCISE 4 *Backing up your requests with logical consequences*

Think of some logical consequences for the following situations and make a note of what you would say to your teenager:

Your teenager is playing music too loudly and hasn't followed your request to turn it down.

....

....

....

Your teenager has borrowed their brother's computer game without permission and ignores your request that they should go and ask him.

....

....

....

Your teenager is arguing loudly with a sister about which TV channel to watch and ignores your suggestion that they solve the problem in a friendly and quiet way.

....

....

....

Your teenager borrowed your bike, and despite your request that they put it away, has left it out in the rain.

....

....

....

Acknowledging Teenagers' Emotions

Dealing with teenagers' emotions can be very difficult for parents. Teenagers can become emotional quite quickly when things happen they cannot control. This typically includes being angry, fearful, or sad. Sometimes these emotions are brief and don't require any response by the parent, but at other times they may continue or escalate and need to be dealt with. These occasions are important as they provide opportunities for you to help your teenager learn to cope with the disappointments and frustrations that they will face throughout life. If you have already been doing this during their early years, it will be so much easier as the problems they face get bigger. If this is new to you, it will be more difficult, but that makes it more important than ever that you learn now, while you can still help.

When a teenager seems upset by something, it is best to approach it in two stages: first, acknowledge how they are feeling and see if you can find out why they are upset; after you have done that, then see if you can work out what you might do to help.

Acknowledge the distress

The first thing to do when you become aware that your teenager is distressed is to stop what you are doing and pay attention to your teenager. While your teenager is talking, stay silent, but listen closely to what they are saying. Do not interupt, tell them they are wrong, or try to make them feel better. You may ask a clarifying question if you are having trouble following what they are saying. When they have finished, repeat what you think your teenager has told you, but use your own words. Check with them to see whether you got it right. Try to help your teenager put a name to the feeling — once they have learned to label a feeling accurately, it is easier to talk about and deal with. Reassure your teenager it is okay to feel that way — perhaps share a time when you last felt that way too. Be cautious when labeling your teenager's emotions. It is often better to make tentative suggestions — *Sounds a bit like you're mad at your brother?* This allows the teenager to give a different label if it does not quite fit — *No, it's just that*

I'm disappointed he let me down. It is often difficult trying to put labels on other people's feelings, but if handled with care, it can be very helpful.

Ask if you can help

After reaching this point, and after your teenager has begun to calm down, ask them what they want you to do. This may be to just listen, to help them cope with their current feelings, or perhaps to set a goal for change. If you think they want to problem solve, prompt them through the steps: clarify the goal, select a solution, and come up with a plan to try out (refer back to page 35 for more detail). If your teenager does not respond to your suggestions, or directs their frustration at you, suggest a cooling off period, and perhaps set a time to talk again.

EXERCISE 5 *Preparing to deal calmly with teenagers' emotions*

Think of a recent example when your teenager was distressed about something.

What could you say to your teenager when you notice they are distressed about something?

....

....

What could you say to your teenager to show you are listening?

....

....

What could you say to your teenager to show you understand they are feeling emotional?

....

....

When should you ask your teenager if you can help?

....

....

What could you say to your teenager if they have calmed down and want you to help them sort things out?

....

....

What could you say to your teenager if they have not calmed down or do not want your help?

....

....

Developing Parenting Routines

Sometimes teenagers' emotions are brief and do not require any further action by the parent. At other times these emotional reactions may continue or escalate and need to be dealt with. The flow chart below shows how to put together some strategies to create a routine for dealing with emotional behaviour. This routine is useful when you have to deal with emotional behaviour, particularly if it has resulted from a disagreement with you. This can typically occur when your teenager is trying to avoid doing something you have asked them to do, or when you have refused to let them do something they want to do. By following this routine you can break the escalation trap where parent and teenager become increasingly angry or upset before one or the other gives in or storms off in a temper. It is likely that you will remain calm and your teenager will be less likely to escalate if you follow these steps.

ROUTINE FOR DEALING WITH EMOTIONAL BEHAVIOUR

Points to remember

- When your teenager becomes angry or upset, stop what you are doing if you can, look at them, and just listen to what they are saying.

- Try to pick out the key point or points, and when they pause, summarise what you thought they said — *So what I hear you saying is that you're upset because I won't let you go to the party on the weekend?* Use an enquiring tone, rather than saying it as a statement of fact — this allows your teenager to correct any misunderstanding and shows that you have really been listening.

- Acknowledge, and if possible, name the emotion — *Well I can hear that you're really angry with me and disappointed at missing out on this party.*

- Pause for at least 5 seconds to give your teenager time to calm down. Do not say anything, and especially do not try to solve the problem, or change your mind, or dismiss your teenager's emotions as trivial or unimportant.

- If your teenager calms down, ask what they want you to do — *Is there any way I can help?* Guide them towards problem solving, using the strategy described on pages 34 and 35. Remember that your aim is to help them come up with a solution themselves and not to do it for them. Give them as much help as they need, but no more.

- If the issue is about a decision you have made, your teenager might ask you to change your mind. At this point you have several options.

  (1) You may decide to keep to your original decision, and in this case you might want to discuss how your teenager could take part in an alternative event. For example, if your teenager is disappointed at not going to a party because they will not have a chance to spend time with their friends, perhaps you could suggest a small party at your own home, or some other social event you could help organise. You might find it helpful to review the strategy for providing opportunities for engaging activities that was discussed in Week 2 (page 33).

  (2) You may decide that your teenager could take part in some of the activity they are wanting to attend, but not all of it. For example, you might suggest that you are willing to allow them to go to the party, but insist that they must come home at a certain time and that you will pick them up to ensure this occurs. In order to ensure that you have a clear agreement with your teenager about any arrangement you decide on, you may find it helpful to review the strategy of using a behaviour contract that was discussed in Week 2 (pages 40 to 43).

  (3) The third option is to reconsider whether your original decision was hasty or unreasonable and to now allow them to go. If you choose this option, you must ensure that you make this decision only after a period of calm discussion with your teenager. If you change your mind while your teenager is being emotional, or soon afterwards, they may learn that the way to get you to change your mind is to turn on their emotional behaviour. You may then find this happening more and more often.

- If your teenager does not calm down after you have waited for 5 seconds, simply repeat your acknowledgment, using slightly different words if you can — *Peter, I can see how upset you are about this, you're really angry aren't you?* Then go on and validate the emotion — *I can understand that you're disappointed* — *it's a perfectly natural reaction.* This gives your teenager the message that you are not criticising them for the way they feel and helps them to accept the feeling and separate it from what they might want to do about it.

- It is not possible to talk about a problem calmly and rationally when one person is emotionally aroused. Humans have the ability to respond emotionally when something happens that we do not like, as well as to rationally think through a problem and come up with a solution. However, these are two separate processes and they interfere with each other. If you stay calm and focused on solving a problem, you cannot be angry at the same time. But if you are angry and upset, you cannot focus your thoughts on solving a problem. As the parent, you can help your teenager to learn this by staying calm yourself, and avoiding the escalation trap (see page 7 for a review of the escalation trap).

- After repeating the acknowledgment and validating your teenager's emotions, again pause for at least 5 seconds to give your teenager time to calm down. Do not say anything, and again do not try to solve the problem, change your mind, or dismiss your teenager's emotions as trivial or unimportant.

- If your teenager still does not calm down, suggest that further discussion now will not be useful and a cooling off period is the best option — *You still seem very angry and I don't think we should talk any more until you've calmed down; how about you go to your room for 30 minutes — then we'll try again.*

- Keep to the agreement, and when you meet again, repeat the routine. You would now be hoping to just go down the shorter, right-hand side of the routine and have a calm discussion about what to do.

- If your teenager resists your suggestion to take some time to cool off and tries to insist on discussing the issue while they are still upset, initiate the cooling off period yourself — *Well, I'm now starting to feel angry and I don't want to talk to you while I'm feeling that way so I'm going to take the dog for a walk and I'll talk to you again in 30 minutes when I get back.*

- If your teenager starts to become emotional or aggressive at any point in the routine, follow the flow chart which suggests that you simply repeat the acknowledgment and validate the emotion, and pause for at least 5 seconds.

EXERCISE 6 *Using the routine for dealing with emotional behaviour*

> Now practise this routine before using it with your teenager. This practice exercise can help you decide whether this is a routine you would feel comfortable using with your teenager. It also gives you a chance to practise the words you would actually say to your teenager before having to do so.
>
> Work through the steps of the routine as though you were talking to your teenager. The first time you practise the routine, imagine that your teenager does indeed calm down after you have listened to them and acknowledged the emotion. On the next practice, have the person playing your teenager continue to be angry or upset so that you can practise suggesting a calming down period of time out.
>
> On page 64 are some examples of how to use this routine in some common situations.

Session 3

UPSET BY SOMEONE OUTSIDE THE FAMILY	UPSET BY SOMEONE INSIDE THE FAMILY	UPSET AT YOU	MANIPULATING
Stop what you are doing and listen to what your teenager is saying. When they have finished speaking, paraphrase what you heard them say. Check to make sure you've got it right.	Stop what you are doing and listen to what your teenager is saying. When they have finished speaking, paraphrase what you heard them say. Check to make sure you've got it right.	Stop what you are doing and listen to what your teenager is saying. When they have finished speaking, paraphrase what you heard them say. Check to make sure you've got it right.	Listen to what your teenager is saying. When they have finished speaking, ignore the emotional behaviour, and prompt them to consider other ways to deal with the problem.
Acknowledge and name the emotion — *Sounds like you're really upset that she let you down?*	Acknowledge and name the emotion — *Sounds like you're really angry that Ben took your gear?*	Acknowledge and name the emotion — *You're really mad at me aren't you?*	Suggest that the emotional behaviour is inappropriate — *That isn't going to solve the problem is it?*
If they are very upset, give them time to cool down. Then, perhaps share a similar experience of your own — *I remember the last time that happened to me…*	If they are very upset, suggest they take time to cool down — *Let's talk about how to fix this when you've cooled down a bit?*	If they are very upset, suggest they take time to cool down — *How about we talk about this in a while when you're not so angry?*	If they continue to show emotional behaviour, continue to ignore it. Tell them you will help when they show interest in finding a solution — *I'm ready to help when you want me to.*
When they have calmed down, ask your teenager what they would like you to do — *What do you want me to do?*	When they have calmed down, ask your teenager what they would like you to do — *What do you want me to do?*	When they have calmed down, ask your teenager what they would like you to do — *What do you want me to do?*	If your teenager approaches you about finding a solution, ask them what they want to do — *What do you think you might do?*
If your teenager does not want your help, make an open offer — *If you want to talk about it later, let me know.*	If your teenager does not want your help, make an open offer — *If you want to talk about it later, let me know.*	If your teenager does not want to talk, make an open offer — *If you want to talk about it later, let me know.*	If your teenager does not want your help, make an open offer — *If you want to talk about it later, let me know.*
If your teenager accepts your offer of help, then or later, coach them to problem solve — *Well, what do you want to happen now?*	If your teenager accepts your offer of help, then or later, coach them to problem solve — *Well, what do you want to happen now?*	If your teenager accepts your offer to talk, then or later, coach them to problem solve — *Well, what do you want to happen now?*	If your teenager accepts your offer of help, then or later, coach them to problem solve — *Well, what is it you're supposed to do?*
Praise them for dealing appropriately with their emotions.	Praise them for dealing appropriately with their emotions.	Praise them for dealing appropriately with their emotions.	Praise them for dealing appropriately with their emotions.

Sometimes, teenagers may have learned that emotional behaviour helps them to escape or avoid things they do not want to do. In these situations, it is best to ignore them, or perhaps prompt them to try something more constructive. If the emotional response is directed at you, the parent, the most important thing is to try and stay calm. Once you have listened to your teenager, they may be able to move to problem solving. Sometimes a parent will need to make it very clear on several occasions that the emotional behaviour is not going to help solve the problem, that it is up to the teenager to suggest a better solution, and that you are willing to assist them to problem solve when they are ready.

EXERCISE 7 *Preparing to deal with manipulative behaviour*

Think of recent examples when your teenager may have been using their apparent distress to avoid something, or to get you to do something for them they really should have done themselves. Use the space below to note down what you might have done or said at each of the steps.

What could you say to your teenager if they complain they cannot do something you know they can?

....

....

....

What could you say to your teenager if they ask you to do something that they should really do for themselves?

....

....

....

What could you say to your teenager if they shout at you that you should fix their problem for them?

....

....

....

Use a Behaviour Contract to Manage Problem Behaviour

If your teenager has difficulty following the new rules or controlling their emotions, and directed discussion or these other strategies do not work, you may need to set up a behaviour contract. This will help the new behaviours to become established. Set up a behaviour contract for rule following using the steps discussed in the previous section on encouraging desirable behaviour. Use a family meeting to discuss what the rules will be, and what the rewards will be for following them.

It is often difficult to keep track of rule-following. Rule-breaking is much easier to notice. One way to deal with this problem is to award points in advance on a daily basis, say 3 points per rule per day. If you have 4 rules, this means that your teenager could earn 84 points per week (3 x 4 x 7). Each instance of rule breaking loses 1 point, and these are deducted from the daily or weekly total. Rewards can be negotiated for the points remaining, such as visiting a friend on the weekend (e.g. 10 points), using the 'phone (e.g. 5 points per 15 minutes), going to a movie (e.g. 25 points) and so on. Rule-following thus leads to gaining the rewards, and rule-breaking risks losing them.

Many of the guidelines for using behaviour contracts that were described in the previous section (pages 40 and 41) are still relevant here. You may wish to review them to make sure your contract covers all the important points.

Identify a few family rules that are fair, easy to follow, and can be enforced.

....

....

Choose rewards or privileges that your teenager will enjoy, and that are appropriate for improved rule-following.

....

....

Finally, link following the rules, with the reward or privilege you have agreed with your teenager. Remember to set moderately easy goals at first so your teenager is rewarded for any improvement, then you can gradually make the goals harder to achieve.

....

....

List anything you need to purchase or get organised before you can start using the contract.

....

....

EXERCISE 8 *How to use a behaviour contract to manage problem behaviour*

Look at the two example contracts 2A and 2B on pages 67 and 68 for some ideas that might help improve your contract.

Now you are ready to take your *draft* Behaviour Contract to a family meeting to discuss how it might work, and to see if it can be improved. Discuss any proposed Behaviour Contract with your teenager and anyone else who might be affected.

Between: Peter   and: Mum/Dad

Starting on: Monday August 9th

Rules:

- Be gentle with each other (no hurting)
- Speak quietly (no yelling)
- Respect privacy and personal space (ask first)

Rewards: Points not lost can be exchanged for privileges. Weekly rewards – go to football game = 30pts; family bbq = 20pts; choose Friday night takeaway food = 10pts

Conditions: No credit; Max. of 5 points carried over to next week

EXAMPLE MONITORING CHART #2A

Name: Peter   Week beginning: Monday August 9th

ACTIVITY & DETAILS	CARRY OVER	M	TU	W	TH	F	SA	SU	TOTAL
MAXIMUM POINTS/DAY = 9 Family rules • Be gentle – no hurting • Speak quietly – no yelling • Respect privacy – ask first Points lost/day Points earned/day Points available Points used Carried over									

Between: Peter   and: Mum/Dad

Starting on: Monday August 9th

Rules:

- Be gentle with each other (no hurting)
- Speak quietly (no yelling)
- Respect privacy and personal space (ask first)

Rewards: Points not lost can be exchanged for privileges. Weekly rewards – go to football game = 30pts; family bbq = 20pts; choose Friday night takeaway food = 10pts. Daily rewards – 15 minutes 'phone time = 2pts; 15 minutes later to bed = 2pts; 15 minutes playing a card game with parent = 2pts; ice cream for dessert = 2pts

Conditions: No credit; Max. of 5 points carried over to next week.

Points are tallied at 6pm each evening; any points earned after 6pm are credited to next day's total; points may be carried over to the next day, but there is a 60 minute daily maximum on phone calls, card games, or staying up late; if more than 6 rule-breaks occur on any day (6pm to 6pm), all points are frozen and cannot be used that day, although they can be carried over to the next day.

EXAMPLE MONITORING CHART #2B

Name: Peter   **Week beginning:** Monday August 9th

ACTIVITY & DETAILS	CARRY OVER	M	TU	W	TH	F	SA	SU	TOTAL
MAXIMUM POINTS/DAY = 9 Family rules • Be gentle – no hurting • Speak quietly – no yelling • Respect privacy – ask first Points lost/day Points earned/day Points available Points used Carried over									

BEHAVIOUR CONTRACT #2

Between: .... and: ....

Starting on: .... (date)

Rules: ....

....

....

....

Rewards: ....

....

....

Conditions: ....

....

....

....

MONITORING CHART #2

Name: .... Week beginning: ....

ACTIVITY & DETAILS	CARRY OVER	M	TU	W	TH	F	SA	SU	TOTAL
Maximum points/day = Family rules • • • • • *Points lost/day* *Points earned/day* *Points available* *Points used* *Points carried over*									

Family Meeting

Hold another family meeting to discuss the rules, and to plan the behaviour contract.

Will you keep to the same time you set for last week's meeting? If not, think about what might be a better time. What else could you do to improve the running of the meeting?

....

....

....

....

CONCLUSION

In today's session, six strategies for managing teenagers' problem behaviour were introduced. These included:

- clear family rules
- directed discussion
- clear, calm requests
- logical consequences
- dealing with teenagers' emotions
- behaviour contracts.

Think about which of these strategies you would like to use with your teenager.

- Choose 1 or 2 strategies (other than the behaviour contract) for managing problem behaviour we considered in this session that you would like to try out with your teenager. Use the checklist on page 72 of your Workbook (an additional copy of this form is provided in the Worksheets section at the end).

- Write down the 2 strategies you plan to use over the next 7 days.

....

....

....

- Hold a family meeting to discuss and put into practice Behaviour Contract #1 for increasing teenager behaviour (chores) you designed in Session 2, and discussed at the beginning of today's session. An example agenda for the family meeting is provided on page 73. Also, discuss the family rules you plan to introduce and set up a draft Behaviour Contract #2 with your teenager and other family members (use the blank form on page 74). However, do not start using it with your teenager until after the next session which will provide more information.

- Continue monitoring the problem behaviour you selected at the end of Session 1.

- Complete any unfinished exercises from today's session.

For a review of the material covered in today's session, you may like to read:

- Session 3 of *Teen Triple P Group Workbook*

or watch:

- *Every Parent's Guide to Teenagers*, Part 4, Managing Problem Behaviour.

Content of Next Session

Session 4 will look at dealing with risky situations in which a teenager's behaviour can be particularly difficult to manage. You will also be introduced to family survival tips to help make the task of parenting easier.

CHECKLIST FOR MANAGING PROBLEM BEHAVIOUR

Choose two of the strategies discussed in Session 3 which you would like to practice with your teenager over the next week. Be as specific as possible (e.g. one goal may be to make clear calm requests with your teenager at least once per day). Use the table below to record whether you reached your goals each day. Comment on what went well and list any problems that occurred.

GOAL 1:
....

....

GOAL 2:
....

....

DAY	GOAL 1 Y/N	GOAL 2 Y/N	COMMENTS
1			
2			
3			
4			
5			
6			
7			

PLAN AND HOLD FAMILY MEETING #2

Preparation

- Agree on time and place for meeting; agree on realistic time-limit (e.g. 30 minutes)
- Gather all relevant material together from noticeboard
- Appoint Chairperson, Timekeeper, & Recorder, etc.

Agenda

- *Item 1·* Discuss Behaviour Contract #1 — Increasing teenager behaviour (chores)
- *Item 2:* Discuss and negotiate draft Behaviour Contract #2 — Family Rules that teenager might agree to.
- *Item 3:* Draw up Monitoring Chart #2
- *Item 4:* Any other business.
- *Item 5:* Set time for next meeting.

Before closing the meeting, quickly review any important decisions that have been made.

Afterwards

Where possible, organise some brief pleasant activity for all family members to do together to reward everyone for taking part in the family meeting.

BEHAVIOUR CONTRACT #2

Between: .... and: ....

Starting on: ....(date)

Rules: ....

....

....

....

Rewards: ....

....

....

....

Conditions:...

....

....

....

MONITORING CHART #2

Name: .... Week beginning: ....

ACTIVITY & DETAILS	CARRY OVER	M	TU	W	TH	F	SA	SU	TOTAL
Maximum points/day = Family rules • • • • • *Points lost per day* *Points earned per day* *Points available* *Points used* *Points remaining/carried*									

Dealing With Risky Behaviour

OVERVIEW

As teenagers spend more time with people away from home, they may develop opinions that differ from those of their parents. They may also experiment more and take unacceptable risks. This can lead to conflict at home, especially if parents try and restrict these activities. Discussions on these topics can often become unpleasant and destructive. Parents sometimes try to restrict their teenager's activities, not because of the activity itself, but because of concern and fear about what else might happen to them. Certainly some of these fears are real, but others may be blown out of proportion by the media. The challenge for parents is to help educate their teenager so that they recognise risky situations, avoid them if possible, and escape from those that cannot be avoided. In today's session, you will also look at family survival tips to help make parenting easier.

OBJECTIVES

By the end of Session 4, you should be able to:

- identify situations that may put your teenager's health or wellbeing at risk
- describe the six steps involved in designing a routine to deal with risky behaviour (i.e. plan ahead, talk about concerns and risks, select risk-reduction strategies, use rewards for appropriate behaviour, use back-up consequences for inappropriate behaviour, and hold a follow-up review)
- construct a community contact network to help monitor your teenager's behaviour.

- use the family survival tips to help make the task of parenting easier.

You will also be expected to:

- be available and prepared for telephone consultation sessions once a week for the next three weeks.
- call your 'buddy' at least once a week to offer support and discuss progress.

ACTIVITIES

High Risk Situations

EXERCISE **1** *Identifying high-risk situations*

Place a tick next to those situations listed below which might be high-risk times for your family. There is a space at the bottom of the table for you to add any additional high-risk situations.

SITUATION	COMMENTS
☑ Visiting friends	
☐ Going to parties	
☑ Going off with friends (e.g. camping)	
☐ School holidays	
☑ Going out at night (e.g. movies)	
☑ Weekends	
☑ On the way to or home from school	
☐ Travelling on public transport	
☐ Going to local stores, shopping centre, etc.	
☐ After school	
☐ Alone at home	
☐	
☐	
☐	

- where they are place?
- with who they are?
- what time you be home?

Routine for Dealing With Risky Behaviour

Many teenagers are tempted to smoke, drink alcohol, miss school, or join their peers in other risky activities. They may want to drop commitments that are demanding, such as sports training, music practice, or even homework. This is partly because the natural rewards for resisting temptation or persisting with a difficult task are usually delayed. In contrast, the rewards for giving in to temptation are usually immediate and powerful, especially if provided by peers. There can also often be unpleasant consequences for *not* joining in with their peers, such as social isolation, teasing, and bullying.

Planning ahead for high-risk situations can avoid many problems. The recommended strategy involves problem solving ahead of time to prevent serious problems from occurring. The main idea is to anticipate risky activities that your teenager may wish to be involved in. By being clear about what you want your teenager to do to reduce or avoid risk, you can prevent most problems from occurring.

The routine for dealing with risky behaviour requires you to follow these steps:

Identify high-risk situations

If you can do this in advance, you avoid being put under pressure to make a decision without having time to think through the details. Often talking to other parents or older teenagers will help you anticipate difficult times ahead. Going to sleep-overs, parties, late movies; driving around with older teenagers, or hanging out at the shopping center — these are a few situations where teenagers can be exposed to risk and temptation. Think about what your teenager is likely to want to go to and what your response is going to be. You do not want them being exposed to risks they cannot manage, but nor do you want to prevent them from having fun with their friends.

Do some advanced planning

Decide whether you need to obtain information before you sit down to talk with your teenager. You may want to find out about public transport, movie locations and screening times, phone cards, taxi company phone numbers, and other parents' phone numbers. Sometimes you will want your teenager to do some of this work; on other occasions it pays to be prepared. You can always get them to obtain the information, even if you know it already! They need to take responsibility for obtaining information about things they want to do. You may have to help them locate information sources — but they should obtain the information themselves if they can.

Talk about concerns and risks

Your teenager needs to understand your concerns, and the risks you have identified you want to reduce or avoid. Find a time to talk together when you will not be interrupted. Explain why you are concerned about their going to a late night movie or party (e.g. drugs, sex, alcohol). Tell them you are willing to allow them to go if you can be assured they will not get into trouble, and that together you want to come up with some rules that they will follow. They may protest that your fears are groundless and you are over-reacting. Unless they can prove to your satisfaction that they are correct, you should insist that it is your concerns that need to be addressed, and you are not prepared to let them attend unless they have a plan you are happy with.

Select risk reduction strategies

Decide on rules for appropriate behaviour in the situation and discuss them calmly with your teenager. These include details such as what time to be home, and what to do if something unexpected happens, like missing the last bus. Problem-solve with your teenager to come up with the best plan you can between you. Refer back to the problem solving steps on page 35 if necessary. You need to be satisfied that your teenager has a plan to deal with events you are concerned about, even though they may protest that they will never happen. If your teenager protests that it is not worth going under the conditions you impose, point out that if it works out okay this time, you will review it for next time. They can take it or leave it. Immediately before the risky situation occurs, ask your teenager to repeat the rules — *So what did we decide you should do after the movie is over?; What did we decide you would do if the others start smoking dope?*

Reward appropriate behaviour

If your teenager sits down with you and works out a satisfactory agreement they should be rewarded by gaining limited access to activities and events they want — this way a compromise can be negotiated to satisfy everyone. Sometimes an additional reward for keeping to the plan might be appropriate. For example, if your teenager reliably comes home on time from the movie on Friday night, they might get to go to a highly desired event, such as an important sporting event or music concert.

Specify a back-up consequence

This acts as a deterrent to discourage risky behaviour. This may be necessary because parental approval and other rewards for keeping to the plan can sometimes be over-shadowed by those on offer from peers and peer-related activities. For a back-up consequence to be effective as a deterrent it needs to be fairly important to your teenager. It must be something you are willing to impose if you have to — do not pick a consequence you would not ever be able or willing to impose. However, do not pick one that is so severe your teenager might avoid coming home because of it. Often teenagers will be confident that they will follow the rules and will suggest appropriate consequences themselves. Avoid consequences that work against other goals or contracts.

Hold a follow-up review session after the event

This allows you both to review how well the plan worked, and to modify it if necessary for next time. In this discussion, which should be held fairly soon after the event, the aim is to praise any successes, and if necessary, briefly and calmly describe any part of the plan that the teenager forgot, or that did not work well. If necessary, return to problem solving to revise the plan for next time a similar event occurs. If you had to impose a consequence because of a failure to follow the agreed plan, discuss how and when your teenager might be allowed to try again. Remember your goal should be to assist your teenager to behave appropriately in risky situations. Preventing them from going to such activities at all does not allow them to learn these skills, and sets up resentment and conflict that can lead to serious family break-down in the long run.

A sample routine for a teenager wanting to go to a late-night movie on a Friday night is presented on page 79. This shows how all the steps fit together to make a routine for dealing with risky behaviour.

Not take healthy thing, or field trip as
Punshiment.

EXAMPLE ROUTINE FOR DEALING WITH RISKY BEHAVIOUR

Wanting to go to a late-night movie and then a coffee shop afterwards

IDENTIFY THE HIGH-RISK SITUATION

- Engaging in antisocial or drug use behaviour after attending a late-night movie on Friday night

LIST ANY ADVANCED PLANNING OR PREPARATION

- Check movie screening times
- Check with parents of peers to see if they share your concerns, and what they are planning, if anything – you may be able to combine plans

TALK ABOUT CONCERNS AND RISKS

- Friends pressuring teenager to 'join in' or 'just try it'
- Missing last bus home and being at risk of abduction or attack
- Using drugs or alcohol and being taken advantage of sexually

SELECT RISK REDUCTION STRATEGIES

- If her friends choose to go to a bar instead of the coffee shop, she will go to the coffee shop on her own
- If there is no one she knows in the coffee shop, she will come straight home
- She will phone parents from the coffee shop when she arrives
- In any case, she will catch the 11.30 bus and be home by midnight
- She will take change for the phone or a cell phone plus the fare for the bus
- She will check the bus times on her way in, and work out in advance how long it takes to walk from the coffee shop to the bus stop.

AGREE ON A REWARD FOR APPROPRIATE BEHAVIOUR

- Praise and approval for any participation in selecting risk reduction strategies
- Special event on Saturday, perhaps with a parent (e.g. trip to a sporting event, going to the beach or shopping)
- Points toward a larger more distant reward (e.g. computer game, new clothes)

SPECIFY A BACKUP CONSEQUENCE FOR PROBLEM BEHAVIOUR

- Penalty for not keeping to the plan – not permitted to go out at night to social events for the next 2 weeks
- Loss of points toward larger reward
- No special event on Saturday

LIST INFORMATION/ITEMS REQUIRED TO MAKE THE PLAN WORK

- Times of buses coming home late on Friday night
- Check out how long it takes to walk from the coffee shop to the bus stop
- Enough money for bus fare and phone call

HOLD A FOLLOW-UP DISCUSSION TO EVALUATE HOW WELL THE PLAN WORKED

(carried out after the event)

– clear rules very important.

4
Session

EXERCISE 2 *Developing a routine for dealing with risky behaviour*

Now you have the chance to design your own routine. In small groups, work through a risky situation of your choice.

DEALING WITH RISKY BEHAVIOUR

Identify the risky situation

....

List any advance planning or preparation

....

....

....

Discuss concerns and risks

....

....

....

Select risk reduction strategies using problem-solving method

....

....

....

List rewards for appropriate behaviour

....

....

....

List backup consequences for problem behaviour

....

....

....

List information/items required to make the plan work

....

....

....

Family Survival Tips

It is easier to look after your teenager's needs if you also look after your own. Here are some more ideas that can help make parenting easier.

Work as a team

Parenting is easier when both parents (where applicable) and other caregivers agree on methods of discipline. Parents should support and back up each other's parenting efforts. Before you use new strategies, discuss the plan with your partner and consult your teenager.

Avoid arguments in front of your teenager

All children are very sensitive to adult conflict. They become distressed if arguments occur often and are not resolved. If you have a major disagreement, try to discuss it at a time when your teenager is not present. Parents sometimes think that teenagers are not affected by parental conflict, but they usually just show it less, or in unexpected ways. If these issues are not addressed, they can cause considerable problems for teenagers, especially in developing their own relationships.

Get support

Everyone needs support in raising teenagers. Partners, family, friends and neighbours can provide good support. Talk about your ideas and compare experiences. This is particularly important with teenagers. Parents are often unsure about how much freedom to allow, and can be swayed by comments like — *All my friends' parents are letting them go to the party!* This may be true — and it may not. Take the time to ring a few parents and find out. If you do not know any parents of your teenager's friends, make it your business to get to know them, at least so you can 'phone occasionally and check out claims like these.

It is also important to be confident about where your teenager is, and what they are doing. Teenagers need to earn their parents' trust, and it is quite appropriate for parents to check on what they are told. Phoning the parents of the friend they are supposed to be spending the evening with, or asking for details of the movie or show they were supposed to be watching shows that you care about them. You need to know where they are in case something goes wrong and they do not come home on time, or if you need to contact them over an emergency. As trust is demonstrated, you will need to check less, but this should not be taken for granted. Teenagers often get into trouble because they did not anticipate what might happen in a new situation. Having their parents know where they are can be a vital factor in avoiding serious problems.

Have a break

Everyone needs some time away from their teenagers. This is normal and healthy. As your teenagers become more skilled and trustworthy, you will be able to leave them at home alone, or with friends, perhaps for an evening at first, and later for longer periods. A discreet phone call to the house or to the neighbours may be used to reassure yourself that all is well. If things do not quite go as well as you hoped, impose an appropriate consequence, problem solve how to do it better next time, and then provide another opportunity at an appropriate time.

EXERCISE 3 *Developing a parent and community network*

You may like to continue to meet with other group participants. Talk to members of the group and identify someone who can be a "buddy" that you can call regularly for support.

My nominated buddy is (name and telephone number).

....

We agree to telephone each other at least once per week. A good time to contact each other is..

Now, write down the name, identity, and phone number of anyone you know who could help you to monitor your teenager.

NAME	IDENTITY / POSITION	PHONE NUMBER(S)

If you know the parents of some of your teenager's friends, you are in a better position to monitor your teenager's behaviour. Monitoring does not need to be intrusive or a threat to your teenager's independence. It needs to be a natural part of your problem solving, risk-management planning. It tells your teenager you care about them, and helps family members keep in touch.

Preparing for Telephone Sessions

The next part of the program consists of individual telephone sessions with your group leader. The aim is to provide you with personal assistance in dealing with any remaining issues or concerns about your teenager's behaviour. Your responsibilities for the telephone sessions include being available for the telephone call each week at the set time, and contacting the group facilitator ahead of time to reschedule the appointment if you know you will not be available for their call. If your telephone is busy or you are unavailable when your group facilitator calls, they will not call again until the next week — it is up to you to call them and schedule another appointment. Telephone sessions will finish after 3 weeks no matter how many sessions you have completed in that time.

EXERCISE 4 *Choosing a time*

> Your group leader will nominate times for telephone sessions. Make a note of the time you have been allocated.
> I will be available for my telephone session with
>
> ....
>
> each week for the next three weeks on (day) ....
>
> at (time) ....

CONCLUSION

Summary of Session

In today's session, seven steps for planning a routine for risky situations were discussed:

- prepare in advance
- talk about concerns and risks
- select risk reduction strategies
- use rewards to encourage appropriate behaviour
- use back-up consequences for problem behaviour
- list information/items required to make the plan work
- hold a follow-up discussion.

In addition, family survival tips were introduced to help make the task of parenting easier. You have also prepared for your telephone sessions and found a buddy to contact for support. Try to contact your buddy at least once a week to share your experiences and support each other's parenting efforts.

■ TASKS TO COMPLETE BEFORE FIRST TELEPHONE SESSION

- Write down the risky situation you plan to work on this week.

....

....

....

....

- Hold family meeting #3 (see example agenda on page 85). Review Behaviour Contract #1; discuss and implement Behaviour Contract #2; and then choose a high-risk situation and develop a routine. There is a blank Monitoring Chart on page 88 which you may like to use in the future for monitoring any contracts. Try out your routine in the coming week if the opportunity arises. There is a blank 'Dealing with risky behaviour' routine form on page 86, and an evaluation form on page 87. To complete the evaluation form, write down any problems or difficulties you had with any of the steps of your routine and whether the steps helped in reducing the risk. Additional copies of these forms are in the Worksheets section.

- Continue monitoring the behaviour you selected in Session 1.

- Complete any unfinished exercises from Session 4.

- Prepare the agenda for the first telephone session (Exercise 1 and 2 page 90).

For a review of the material covered in today's session, read:

- *Teen Triple P Group Workbook*
  Session 4, Dealing with risky behaviour

or watch:

- *Every Parent's Guide to Teenagers, Part 5*, Dealing with risky behaviour.

Content of Next Session

The next session is the first of your three telephone consultations. In each of the telephone sessions your homework tasks will be reviewed as well as any other issues that you would like to discuss. Please plan ahead for these sessions and consider possible agenda topics before the scheduled session time. It is also suggested that you contact your 'buddy' once a week to offer support and encouragement to one another on your parenting efforts.

PLAN AND HOLD FAMILY MEETING #3

Preparation

- Agree on time and place for meeting; agree on realistic time-limit (e.g. 30 minutes)
- Gather all relevant material together from noticeboard
- Appoint Chairperson, Timekeeper, and Recorder, etc.

Agenda

- *Item 1*: Discuss Behaviour Contract #1 and agree on any changes as necessary
- *Item 2*: Discuss Behaviour Contract #2 and agree to implement it
- *Item 3*: Negotiate risky behaviour plan
- *Item 4*: Any other business
- *Item 5*: Set time for next meeting

Before closing the meeting, quickly review any important decisions that have been made.

Afterwards

Where possible, organise some brief pleasant activity for all family members to do together to reward everyone for taking part in the family meeting.

4

Session

DEALING WITH RISKY BEHAVIOUR

Identify the risky situation

....

List any advance planning or preparation

....

....

....

....

Discuss concerns and risks

....

....

....

Select risk reduction strategies using problem-solving method

....

....

....

List rewards for appropriate behaviour

....

....

....

List backup consequences for problem behaviour

....

....

....

List information/items required to make plan work

....

....

....

After the event: note any goals from the follow-up discussion

....

....

....

CHECKLIST FOR DEALING WITH RISKY BEHAVIOUR ROUTINE

Risky situation: _____

Instructions: Write down any problems you encountered working through the routine with your teenager. Then write down opposite, whether the steps helped to reduce the risk

STEPS FOLLOWED	COMMENTS
1. Advanced planning	
2. Discussing concerns	
3. Selecting risk-reduction strategies	
4. Rewards	
5. Back-up consequences	
6. Information/items required	
7. New goals	

4

Session

MONITORING CHART

Name: .... Week beginning: ....

ACTIVITY & DETAILS	CARRY OVER	M	TU	W	TH	F	SA	SU	TOTAL
Maximum points/day = • • • • • •									
Points lost per day *Points earned per day* *Points available* *Points used per day* *Points remaining/carried*									
Daily rewards • • • • • • Weekly rewards • • • • • •									

Implementing Parenting Routines 1

Session 5

OVERVIEW

This is the first of your three telephone consultation sessions. These sessions are designed to help you continue to put into practice the strategies introduced in Sessions 1 to 4. During this session we will also review how successful you have been in planning routines for dealing with risky behaviour. The remainder of the session will address any current issues or concerns you have.

OBJECTIVES

By the end of Session 5, you should be able to:

- set a clear, specific agenda for future sessions
- set goals and tasks independently
- plan, use, monitor, and modify behaviour contracts as required
- plan, use and evaluate routines for dealing with risky situations as required
- access information on parenting issues, if needed
- get support from family, other parents, and group members when needed.

Preparing for the Session

EXERCISE 1 *Set the agenda (Complete BEFORE the session starts)*

Think about the issues you would like to discuss during your telephone consultation session. Use the space below to list some possible topics for discussion.

....

....

....

....

....

....

....

Update on Progress

EXERCISE 2 *Review tasks set after last session (Complete BEFORE the session starts)*

What were your chosen tasks?

....

....

What worked? Please be specific and think of at least two positive points.

....

....

Is there anything that you could have done differently?

....

....

What do you feel you need to practise?

....

....

Other Issues

Use the space below to make notes about any other agenda items that are discussed during your telephone consultation session.

Summary of Session

List the main points discussed in today's session that require follow up by you. Include any new or revised goals you wish to achieve.

....

....

....

....

■ TASKS TO BE COMPLETED BETWEEN SESSIONS

Write down your tasks for the coming week.

....

....

....

....

■ OPTIONAL TASKS

Write down any material that you feel you need to review this week.

....

....

....

....

Content of Next Session

Before the next telephone consultation, think about the main issues you would like to discuss and write them in the space on page 94 for Exercise 1. Also complete Exercise 2.

Implementing Parenting Routines 2

OVERVIEW

The content of this session will be determined by you. Plan ahead for your session and identify the main issues you would like to discuss.

OBJECTIVES

By the end of Session 6, you should be able to:

- set a clear, specific agenda for future sessions
- set goals and tasks independently
- plan, use, monitor, and modify behaviour contracts as required
- plan, use and evaluate routines for dealing with risky situations as required
- access information on parenting issues, if needed
- get support from family, other parents, and group members when needed
- solve any parenting problems with minimal help from the group leader.

Preparing for the Session

EXERCISE 1 *Set the agenda (Complete BEFORE the session starts)*

Think about the issues you would like to discuss during your telephone consultation session. Use the space below to list some possible topics for discussion.

....

....

....

....

....

....

....

Update on Progress

EXERCISE 2 *Review tasks set after last session (Complete BEFORE the session starts)*

What were your chosen tasks?

....

....

What worked? Please be specific and think of at least two positive points.

....

....

Is there anything that you could have done differently?

....

....

What do you feel you need to practise?

....

....

Other Issues

Use the space below to make notes about any other agenda items that are discussed during your telephone consultation session.

Summary of Session

List the main points discussed in today's session that require follow up by
you. Include any new or revised goals you wish to achieve.

....

....

....

....

■ TASKS TO BE COMPLETED BETWEEN SESSIONS

Write down your tasks for the coming week.

....

....

....

....

■ OPTIONAL TASKS

Write down any material that you feel you need to review this week.

....

....

....

....

Content of Next Session

Before the next telephone consultation, think about the main issues you would like to
discuss and write them in the space on page 98 for Exercise 1. Also complete Exercise 2.

Implementing Parenting Routines 3

EMOTIONAL BEHAVIOUR

Session 7

OVERVIEW

The content of this session will be determined by you. Plan ahead for your session and identify the main issues you would like to discuss.

OBJECTIVES

By the end of Session 7, you should be able to:

- set a clear, specific agenda for future sessions
- set goals and tasks independently
- plan, use, monitor, and modify behaviour contracts as required
- plan, use and evaluate routines for dealing with risky situations as required
- access information on parenting issues, if needed
- get support from family, other parents, and group members when needed
- solve any parenting problems with minimal help from the group leader.

Preparing for the Session

EXERCISE 1 *Set the agenda (Complete BEFORE the session starts)*

Think about the issues you would like to discuss during your telephone consultation session. Use the space below to list some possible topics for discussion.

....

....

....

....

....

....

....

....

Update on Progress

EXERCISE 2 *Review tasks set after last session (Complete BEFORE the session starts)*

What were your chosen tasks?

....

....

What worked? Please be specific and think of at least two positive points.

....

....

Is there anything that you could have done differently?

....

....

What do you feel you need to practise?

....

....

7

Session

Other Issues

Use the space below to make notes about any other agenda items that are discussed during your telephone consultation session.

Summary of Session

List the main points discussed in today's session that require follow up by
you. Include any new or revised goals you wish to achieve.

....

....

....

....

■ TASKS TO BE COMPLETED BETWEEN SESSIONS

Write down your tasks for the coming week.

....

....

....

....

■ OPTIONAL TASKS

Write down any material that you feel you need to review this week.

....

....

....

....

Content of Next Session

Before the final group session, think about the main issues you would like to discuss
and write them in the space on page 102 for Exercise 1.

Program Close

OVERVIEW

This session looks at ways to maintain the changes you have made during the program. Keeping up these improvements over the long term is important. You will also review your family's progress through Group Teen Triple P, and consider high-risk situations that might occur in the near future. Quality family life requires continued effort and parents need to be on the lookout for signs that things might be beginning to slip. At the end of the session, you will complete a booklet of questionnaires like the one you did at the start of the program. These forms help show what changes have occurred in both your own and your teenager's behaviour as a result of completing Group Teen Triple P.

OBJECTIVES

After completing Session 8, you should be able to:

- design, implement and evaluate (i) appropriate parenting strategies to improve desirable behaviour and manage problem behaviour with your teenager, and (ii) routines to assist your teenager deal with potentially risky situations
- use information resources independently
- obtain support from family, friends, and group members, as well as from your parent support network
- solve parenting problems independently

- identify changes in your teenager's and your own behaviour since commencing Group Teen Triple P
- maintain changes made so far in your teenager's and your own behaviour
- set further goals for change in your teenager's and your own behaviour and decide how to achieve these goals.

ACTIVITIES

Update on Progress

EXERCISE 1 *Review tasks set after last session*

What were your chosen tasks?

....

....

What worked?

....

....

Is there anything that you could have done differently?

....

....

What might you need to practise further?

....

....

Family Survival Tips

Take a few minutes to remember the family survival tips that were introduced in Session 4. These are covered in detail on page 81 of this Workbook. They are briefly listed here again.

- work as a team
- avoid arguments in front of your teenager
- get support
- have a break.

Who do your rely on for support?

Family? ....

....

Friends? ....

....

What can you do to increase your support network, if needed?

....

....

....

Make a note of things you like to do (on your own or with your partner or friends) that you have not done for a while, or as regularly as you would like.

....

....

....

Think about how you could have a break or do some of things you listed above.

....

....

....

....

Phasing Out the Program

During the course of this program, a number of things have been introduced into your family's life that are unusual — things that would probably not occur naturally. Examples include homework tasks, keeping records of your own and your teenager's behaviour, and reading the program materials. Finishing a program like this involves stopping these activities. However, this does not mean going back to all you were doing before starting the program. The aim at this stage is to phase out these unusual activities without falling back into the old patterns which were contributing to the problems you were experiencing with your teenager. A number of steps are suggested below to help you do this.

8
Session

Put away the program materials

Put the program materials away somewhere where they are easy to find so that you can pull them out to look at from time to time. You may choose to mark or take out those sections of the program materials that have been the most useful so they are easy to find if you need them.

Phase out monitoring

Throughout the program you have been asked to keep records or to monitor what you have been doing and what your teenager has been doing. In everyday life, most people do not keep ongoing records of their own or their teenager's behaviour. If you are currently keeping records of your progress, decide how well established your new behaviours are. If you feel you can continue your new behaviour without keeping a record, it is time to stop recording. If you are less certain, start to phase out the recording. Monitor your own or your teenager's behaviour less often, such as once a week rather than each day and aim to phase monitoring out altogether when you feel confident of your progress.

Phase out specific strategies

Look at the type of strategies you have in place, such as behaviour contracts. Decide whether these can be simplified and phased out over time. Some of the suggestions we have made, such as praising a teenager frequently for a particular behaviour are most useful for *changing* behaviour. For *maintaining* behaviour it is best to reward behaviours unpredictably from time to time, and not every time the behaviour occurs.

Make changes to behaviour contracts and the use of rewards gradually. Make sure there are still plenty of rewarding things in your teenager's life, and that you look for opportunities to spend time together doing things that you both enjoy. Behaviour problems can reappear if teenagers do not get enough encouragement and support for appropriate behaviour.

Hold regular reviews of progress

During this program, you have attended to your family's problems on a daily or weekly basis. This can be reduced now. However, it is important to keep up with how your family is going. You might wish to keep the family meetings going once every two weeks, or once a month. This allows you to review any problems that might be occurring and to address them before things become serious.

Progress Review

When you began Group Teen Triple P, you identified changes you wanted to see in your teenager's behaviour as well as in your own behaviour.

EXERCISE 3 *Identifying changes that have been made*

Take a few minutes to complete the table below, outlining the changes that both you and your teenager have made since commencing the program. It may be helpful to look back at your goals on page 15 of this Workbook.

CHANGES IN YOUR TEENAGER'S BEHAVIOUR	CHANGES IN YOUR OWN BEHAVIOUR

Session 8

Maintaining Changes

Here are some suggestions for maintaining the improvements you have made. There are five key steps to maintaining change and avoiding lapses.

Identification of potential high-risk situations

An effective way of avoiding future problems involves planning to deal with potentially difficult times before any trouble starts. Just as you plan how to use strategies to encourage appropriate behaviour and manage problem behaviour, you need to plan for future situations where problems may arise. This process can start now. Think of any high-risk situations that are likely to occur in the next few months and try to problem solve ways of dealing with these situations to minimise problems. Some common high-risk times include:

- changes in family structure (separation; new relationship; merging families)
- changes in family financial status
- changes in parental employment status
- times when parents are feeling depressed
- times of marital conflict
- moving house
- renovating or building a house
- changing schools
- exam times
- problems with friends, either same-sex or opposite sex
- death or illness in the family
- involvement in court action.

Early identification of existing problems

It is important to take immediate action if things are not going well. You may decide to restart specific management programs such as behaviour contracts, or go back to the reading material to check strategies or look for new ideas.

Holding regular reviews of progress

If you review your family's progress on a regular basis it is more likely that you will be able to detect any problems as they arise. You will also be able to take appropriate action to prevent any lapses. You may wish to keep the family meetings going to deal with regular events as well as problems. But in any case, review progress every two weeks at first, then at least once a month.

Experimenting with new strategies

If existing strategies are no longer effective, try out new things. Look to what you already know — give your teenager lots of attention and encouragement when they are behaving well and review how you are responding when they misbehave. Try to find ways of adapting existing strategies to the new situation. Give the new way a go for 10 to 14 days, monitor how successful it is, and continue or re-evaluate as appropriate.

Talk to other parents

Don't feel you have to deal with issues on your own. Most parents of teenagers have similar problems, though not always at the same time or in the same order. Build up your network of parents so that everyone can benefit from each other's experiences and successes.

Problem Solving for the Future

EXERCISE 4 *Planning for future high-risk situations*

Spend a few minutes planning possible solutions to these situations. Then discuss your ideas with the group and make additional notes if you like about what you would do if ...

> Your 14-year-old has been in trouble the last three weekends at a team sport (e.g. basketball, baseball, cricket, soccer) for yelling at team-mates and for throwing their bat or ball in anger if they messed up. You are worried they will be thrown off the team if their anger outbursts continue.

> Your 13-year-old is being teased and possibly bullied at school. They do not appear to have any close friends and report that they are being excluded from social groups and activities. They are coming home after school very upset and often complain of feeling sick in the mornings before school. They seem to believe the situation is hopeless, and complain that no one will ever like them and that they will never be any good at anything.

The school holidays start in three weeks time. You have to work most of
the time and you are concerned what your 15-year-old might get up to. You
are also worried they will be bored and irritable and this will lead to more
family squabbles and conflict.

....

....

....

....

....

....

EXERCISE 5 *Identifying future high-risk situations*

Now turn to future high-risk situations that might occur for your teenager.

Write down any high-risk events or situations which you think might occur
in the next six months or so (e.g. going to a new school; starting to date;
experimenting with alcohol, cigarettes, or drugs). List them below.

....

....

....

....

....

....

EXERCISE 6 *Independent problem solving*

The final step is to do some planning of your own.

Use the blank form on page 109 to devise a routine for dealing with one of
the potential high-risk situations you have just identified.

DEALING WITH RISKY BEHAVIOUR

Identify the risky situation

....

List any advance planning or preparation

....

....

....

....

Discuss concerns and risks

....

....

....

Select risk reduction strategies using problem-solving method

....

....

....

List rewards for appropriate behaviour

....

....

....

List backup consequences for problem behaviour

....

....

....

List information/items required to make the plan work

....

....

....

After the event: Note any goals from the follow-up discussion

....

....

Future Goals

EXERCISE **7** *Identifying future goals*

Spend a few minutes now thinking about any other goals you have relating
to your parenting skills and your teenager's behaviour. Discuss your goals
with the group and make additional notes in the space below.

....

....

....

....

....

....

Final Assessment

EXERCISE **8** *Completing Assessment Booklet Two*

Now that you have completed the program, your group facilitator will give
you a copy of *Assessment Booklet Two* to complete. These are the same
forms you completed at the start of the program. The aim is to assess what
changes have occurred during the program and whether the program has
met your family's needs. Please take some time to complete the questionnaires, thinking about how things are at the moment.

....

....

....

....

....

....

Summary of Session

Today's session was used to review your progress through the program and to remind you of the family survival tips to help make parenting easier. We also discussed how to maintain the changes made, how to prevent problems in future high-risk situations, and you also set some goals for the future.

■ HOMEWORK TASKS

- Put your Group Teen Triple P materials away somewhere handy and start to phase out any monitoring records or checklists you may be using.
- Continue to use your positive parenting strategies and your parenting routines for risky situations.

Make a note of any other homework tasks or reading you intend to complete.

....

....

....

....

....

....

Congratulations

You have now completed Group Teen Triple P. Congratulations on staying motivated and interested throughout the program. We hope that you are enjoying the benefits of positive parenting and continue using these strategies. As your teenager continues to grow, different situations and new problems are bound to arise. Refer back to this *Teen Triple P Group Workbook* at any time to review the strategies you have learned or to look up guidelines for dealing with a new problem behaviour. Congratulations for participating in Group Teen Triple P. We hope you found it a worthwhile experience.

Worksheets

It is intended that you will make multiple copies of the following worksheets to use with the exercises in your workbook. Remember to keep the originals so you can make additional copies as required.

BEHAVIOUR DIARY

Instructions: List the problem behaviour, when and where it occurred and what happened before and after the event.

Problem Behaviour: _____

Starting Date: _____

PROBLEM EVENT	WHEN AND WHERE DID IT OCCUR?	WHAT OCCURRED BEFORE THE EVENT?	WHAT OCCURRED AFTER THE EVENT?	OTHER COMMENTS

TALLY SHEET

Instructions: Write the day in the first column, then place a tick in the successive square each time the behaviour occurs on that day. Record the total number of episodes for each day in the end column.

Problem Behaviour: _____

Starting Date: _____

DAY	1	2	3	4	5	6	7	8	9	10	11	12	13	14	15	TOTAL

DURATION RECORD

Instructions: Write the day in the first column, then for each separate occurrence of the target behaviour, record how long it lasted in seconds, minutes or hours. Total the times at the end of each day.

Behaviour: _____   Starting Date: _____

DAY	SUCCESSIVE EPISODES										TOTAL
	1	2	3	4	5	6	7	8	9	10	

TIME-SAMPLING RECORD

Instructions: Place a tick in the square for the corresponding time period if the target behaviour has occurred at least once.

Behaviour: _____   Starting Date: _____

DAYS	M	T	W	T	F	S	S	M	T	W	T	F	S	S	M	T	W	T	F	S	S
TOTAL																					

(Left margin label: TIME OF DAY)

BEHAVIOUR GRAPH

Instructions: Plot the number of times the behaviour occurs each day by placing an X or circle in appropriate column, then join up the marks for each day.

Behaviour: _____

Month: _____

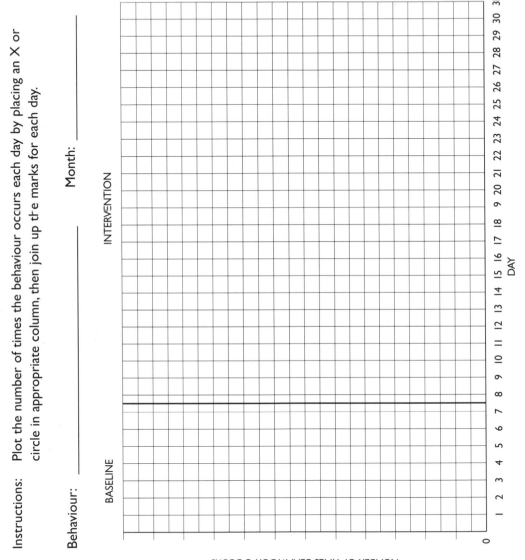

INTERVENTION

BASELINE

NUMBER OF TIMES BEHAVIOUR OCCURS

DAY

CHECKLIST FOR ENCOURAGING APPROPRIATE BEHAVIOUR

Choose two of the strategies discussed during Session 2 or 3 which you would like to practise with your teenager over the next week. Be as specific as possible (e.g. one goal may be to use descriptive praise statements with your teenager at least five times per day). Use the table below to record whether you reached your goals each day. Comment on what went well and list any problems that occurred.

GOAL 1: ....

....

GOAL 2: ....

....

DAY	GOAL 1 Y/N	GOAL 2 Y/N	COMMENTS
1			
2			
3			
4			
5			
6			
7			

DEALING WITH RISKY BEHAVIOUR

Identify the risky situation

....

List any advance planning or preparation

....

....

....

....

Discuss concerns and risks

....

....

....

Select risk reduction strategies using problem-solving method

....

....

....

List rewards for appropriate behaviour

....

....

....

List backup consequences for problem behaviour

....

....

....

List information/items required to make the plan work

....

....

....

After the event: Note any goals from the follow-up discussion

....

....

....

CHECKLIST FOR DEALING WITH RISKY BEHAVIOUR ROUTINE

Risky situation: _____

Instructions: Write down any problems you encountered working through the routine with your teenager. Then write down opposite, whether the steps helped to reduce the risk

STEPS FOLLOWED	COMMENTS
1. Advanced planning	
2. Discussing concerns	
3. Selecting risk-reduction strategies	
4. Rewards	
5. Back-up consequences	
6. Information/items required	
7. New goals	

MONITORING CHART

Name: .... Week beginning: ....

ACTIVITY & DETAILS	CARRY OVER	M	TU	W	TH	F	SA	SU	TOTAL
Maximum points/day = • • • • • •									
Points lost per day *Points earned per day* *Points available* *Points used per day* *Points remaining/carried*									
Daily rewards • • • • • • Weekly rewards • • • • • •									